101 Questions About Dinosaurs

Philip J. Currie
AND
Eva B. Koppelhus

ILLUSTRATIONS BY
Jan Sovak

D1036261

DOVER PUBLICATIONS, INC.
Mineola, New York

Copyright

Text copyright © 1996 by Philip J. Currie and Eva B. Koppelhus.
Illustrations copyright © 1996 by Dover Publications, Inc.
All rights reserved under Pan American and International Copyright Conventions.

Published in Canada by General Publishing Company, Ltd., 30 Lesmill Road, Don Mills, Toronto, Ontario.
Published in the United Kingdom by Constable and Company, Ltd., 3 The Lanchesters, 162–164 Fulham Palace Road, London W6 9ER.

Bibliographical Note

101 Questions About Dinosaurs is a new work, first published by Dover Publications, Inc., in 1996.

Library of Congress Cataloging-in-Publication Data

Currie, Philip J.
    101 questions about dinosaurs   /   Philip J. Currie and Eva B. Koppelhus : illustrations by Jan Sovak.
        p.   cm.
    ISBN 0-486-29172-3 (pbk.)
    1. Dinosaurs—Miscellanea.   I. Koppelhus, Eva B. (Eva Bundgaard)   II. Title.
QE862.D5C86   1996
567.9'1—dc20   96-20786
                                                                                    CIP

Manufactured in the United States of America
Dover Publications, Inc., 31 East 2nd Street, Mineola, N.Y. 11501

Contents

1. General and History

1. What is a dinosaur? Dinosaurs are a type of animal, superficially resembling lizards and crocodiles, that first appeared about 225,000,000 years ago. The earliest dinosaur, like all of its diverse descendants, had a number of characteristics that distinguished it from its contemporaries. Dinosaurs were efficient walkers and runners, and most of the traits that identify them are found in the hind legs. The upper leg bone has a ball-like joint that fits into the hip socket. The outer of the two bones in the lower leg is called the fibula, and it is much thinner than the other lower leg bone, the tibia. And the ankle is peculiar in that the leg joint passes through the mosaic of small bones in such a way that two of the ankle bones have functionally become part of the lower leg. These and other skeletal features are used by scientists to define the Dinosauria. If an extinct animal does not have these characteristics, then it is not a dinosaur. On the other hand, there are some modern animals that have all the characteristics used to define dinosaurs. These are the birds, which have inherited these traits.

With the exception of the birds, all known dinosaurs lived during the Mesozoic era. The Mesozoic is divided into three periods. Dinosaurs appeared 225 million years ago toward the end of the earliest of these periods, known as the Triassic. The Triassic is followed by the Jurassic period (213 to 144 million years ago), when dinosaurs became the dominant land animals throughout the world. The history of dinosaurs is best understood during the last period, the Cretaceous, when they reached the peak of their diversity and evolution.

2. Are extinct marine reptiles (like plesiosaurs and mosasaurs) dinosaurs? Plesiosaurs and mosasaurs are not dinosaurs. When dinosaurs ruled the Earth between 225 and 65 million years ago, there also existed a variety of large, unrelated, marine

1

reptiles. The largest of these were more than 50 feet long. The reptiles that lived in the sea included a number of different types that were not closely related to each other. *Protostega* was a sea turtle with a shell so wide that one could park a truck on it. There were two types of plesiosaurs—those with short necks, and those with long necks. The limbs had been transformed into fish-like paddles, and there can be no doubt about their powerful swimming abilities. Mosasaurs were lizards with paddle–like limbs and a long, powerful swimming tail. Living relatives include varanid lizards like the Komodo dragon. The most specialized marine reptiles were the ichthyosaurs ("fish lizards"). Their body forms were convergent with those of sharks (fish) and porpoises (mammals), and it is doubtful that they could have pulled themselves up on land to walk. Like whales, they probably died quickly when beached.

3. Are pterosaurs (flying reptiles) dinosaurs?   Pterosaurs are not dinosaurs, although these two groups were closely related to each other. The first flying reptiles appeared during Late Triassic times, 225 million years ago, which is about the same time that the first dinosaurs came into being. Flying reptiles (pterosaurs) and dinosaurs are very different types of animals that are easily distinguished from each other. Pterosaurs lasted until the end of the Cretaceous period, when most of the large dinosaurs perished. But they had been declining in numbers and diversity for millions of years before they became extinct. Some of the last pterosaurs were the largest animals known to fly. *Quetzalcoatlus*, first reported from Texas, had a wingspan of more than forty feet.

4. Are birds dinosaurs?   Most people incorrectly assume that dinosaurs are extinct when in fact there are more than 8,000 living species of dinosaurs. Birds are the direct descendants of meat-eating dinosaurs, and under the modern biological classification system they are considered to be a subset of the Dinosauria. The transition from dinosaurs to birds is so well documented in the fossil record that some animals can only be classified as one or the other if the feathers were fossilized. The earliest known fossil bird is *Archaeopteryx* from the Late Jurassic rocks of Germany. With its teeth and long tail, it looks like a small meat-eating dinosaur, and it would never have been identified as a bird if its feathers had not been fortuitously preserved.

5. When was the first dinosaur found? The first dinosaur fossils were probably discovered by people thousands of years ago. In central Asia, dinosaur eggshells were apparently pierced and placed on strings to make jewelry. North American Indians were reputed to have identified dinosaur bones as being from the ancestors of the buffalo (bison). The first historical record of dinosaur bones comes from the Western Jin Dynasty of China. More than 1,500 years ago a Chinese scholar named Chang Qu reported the discovery of dragon bones in a region of Sichuan Province that is now known to be very rich in dinosaur bones. The first well-documented discovery of a dinosaur bone is recorded by a drawing in a book by Robert Plot published in 1677. It is evident from the drawing that the bone was the upper leg bone of a large meat-eating dinosaur called *Megalosaurus*. Although this specimen became the first dinosaur bone with a name (*Scrotum humanum*), it was not recognized as the remains of an extinct animal until long after it had been misplaced and lost. In 1824, *Megalosaurus* became the first dinosaur described and named using essentially modern scientific techniques. Even so, the name "dinosaur" (or more properly, Dinosauria) was not used until 1842, when Sir Richard Owen coined the word.

The first scientific recognition of dinosaurs took place in 1822, when the first specimen of *Iguanodon* was discovered. Mary Anne Mantell noticed a fossilized tooth in a pile of gravel being used for road repairs near London. She showed it to her husband, Dr. Gideon Mantell, who immediately recognized it as being from an unknown plant-eater. It did not receive the name *Iguanodon* until 1825. As mentioned previously, *Megalosaurus* was the first dinosaur given a name that is still used by scientists. The name appeared in print for the first time in 1822 in a book about fossils by James Parkinson. However, the scientific description of this meat-eating dinosaur was not published until two years later by William Buckland.

In North America, dinosaur tracks plowed up in the Connecticut River valley in 1802 by Pliny Moody were originally identified as the footprints of "Noah's Raven." These and other footprints were not recognized as dinosaur tracks until Reverend Edward Hitchcock started studying them in 1835. Dinosaur teeth discovered in 75-million-year-old rocks in Montana were given the names *Deinodon, Trachodon* and *Troodon* by Joseph Leidy in 1856. Unfortunately, only the teeth of *Troodon* were diagnostic enough to be associated with bones from the rest of the skeleton. The first good skeleton was that of a duckbilled dinosaur found near Haddonfield, New Jersey. It was given the name *Hadrosaurus* by Leidy in 1858. Major dinosaur discoveries were made in western North America starting in the 1870s.

6. What was the famous "fossil feud" all about? At the end of the 1870s, two paleontologists became embroiled in a bitter rivalry that led to the discovery and description of many new dinosaurs from western North America. Edward Drinker Cope (1840–1897) from Philadelphia and Othniel Charles Marsh (1831–1899) from Yale University started off as friends, but became so competitive that their "fossil feud" eventually erupted onto the front pages of many of the most influential American newspapers. The intense competition of these two men and their field parties opened up the great fossil fields of the West, and led to the collection of many fine specimens.

7. How long did dinosaurs dominate the world? Dinosaurs are generally divided into two major lineages, referred to as either saurischian (lizard-hipped) or ornithischian (bird-hipped) dinosaurs. These names refer to the arrangement of the three bones in the hips. In lizard-hipped forms, the pubic bone generally slopes down and forward, whereas in bird-hipped dinosaurs the main part of this bone slopes down and backward underneath one of the other hip bones (the ischium). The oldest dinosaurs are from 225-million-year-old rocks in Argentina, but by that time dinosaurs had already divided into both lizard-hipped and bird-hipped forms. Nobody knows how much earlier in time the original dinosaur lived that was the common ancestor of both types. After dinosaurs appeared, they quickly diversified, spread to all continents, and became the dominant land animals. This domination continued for 160 million years, but ended 65 million years ago when most dinosaurs disappeared. Although dinosaurs were the largest animals on land, they would have been outnumbered by their smaller contemporaries, which included lizards, snakes and mammals. As we shall see later, dinosaurs did not all die out 65 million years ago, and the survivors have been so successful that they outnumber mammals!

8. Were dinosaurs the most successful animals? Dinosaurs are considered by many to have been the most successful animals that ever lived. However, success cannot be measured unless the word is defined. There is no doubt that throughout most of the Mesozoic Era, they were the largest animals on land. But the largest dinosaurs are exceeded in weight by the Blue Whale, and many dinosaurs were no larger than chickens. There were many different types of dinosaurs, although only about 500 species are presently known to scientists. It sounds like a lot, but the truth is that there are over 4,000 species of mammals alive today. And there is a high probability that mammals even outnumbered the great dinosaurs during Mesozoic times. So number of species is probably not a good way to define success. Perhaps dinosaurs were the most successful because they lasted longer than other animals? Unfortunately, this does not work either, because the first mammal appears in the fossil record around the same time as the first dinosaur. What we can say is that dinosaurs included the largest land animals that ever walked the Earth, and that for 160 million years they were at the top of the food chain. So even though they never became as numerous as insects nor as large as some whales, they did pretty well in their world.

9. Why is a dinosaur called a dinosaur? Dinosaur means "terrible lizard" and refers to the large size of these animals, which were once thought to be related to lizards and other modern reptiles. By 1841, three types of large extinct reptiles (*Iguanodon*, *Hylaeosaurus* and *Megalosaurus*) had been found in England. They were clearly different from all other known animals, living or dead. The famous English anatomist and paleontologist Sir Richard Owen created a new classification within which these animals could be grouped. "Dinosauria" is derived from two ancient Greek words: "deinos," which means "terrible," and "sauros," which can be translated as "lizard" or "reptile." Dinosaurs, or "terrible lizards," include the longest, tallest, heaviest and perhaps the most ferocious animals that ever walked on land. However, they were not all "terrible." The majority were nonaggressive plant eaters, and many dinosaurs were quite small. And the "terrible lizards" were not lizards at all. In fact, modern paleontologists and biologists even hesitate to call them reptiles.

10.   How do dinosaurs get their names?   Dinosaurs are given their exotic-sounding names by the scientists who find and describe their fossils. The techniques used for constructing the names are the same that are employed by a botanist naming a new species of plant, or a zoologist working on a new species of animal. In all cases, the new name must be one that has not been applied to any other living organism. Usually, an English-speaking person will come up with a name in English, a German will think of a name in German, a Chinese scientist will produce a Chinese name, and so on. A dinosaur can be given a name that describes one of its characteristics, or that creates an impression of what the animal was like, or that is based on where it was found, or that refers to the time when it lived, or that honors the person who discovered it, or that means nothing at all. To avoid the chaos that would result if each one of these names were translated into every language in the world, scientists take the names they invent and translate them into Latin or ancient Greek. These are dead languages that are no longer actively in use. *Tyrannosaurus rex*, which means "tyrant lizard king," is known as *Tyrannosaurus rex* to people in every corner of the world, no matter what language they speak.

11.   Do dinosaurs have common names?   There are several types of common names assigned to dinosaurs. Pet names are sometimes given to individual specimens by the people that find and excavate them. One of the best examples is a *Tyrannosaurus rex* skeleton collected in South Dakota. This specimen, which captured international attention when it was seized by the FBI, has become known around the world as "Sue" (Sue Hendricks was the discoverer). Sometimes the scientific name will be translated from the Latin or ancient Greek into the local language to be used as a popular name. For example, in America *Brontosaurus* is often just referred to as "the thunder lizard." Another technique is to just take the scientific name and modify it slightly so that it conforms more closely to the language of choice. In English, the horned dinosaur *Centrosaurus* could be referred to as a "centrosaur." When the scientific name is modified, it no longer starts with a capital letter, nor is it italicized.

12. Why do some dinosaurs have more than one name? Why, for example, is *Apatosaurus* also called *Brontosaurus*?
Dinosaur species each have only one official name. If a paleontologist is lucky, the fossilized skeleton of a new type of dinosaur will be complete when it is discovered. Many dinosaurs are known from skeletons that are complete from the tip of the nose to the tip of the tail, and include even the delicate little bones in the ears and eyes. In most cases, however, the skeletons were partially destroyed by scavengers or weathering before they were buried, or were broken up as the rocks that encased them were broken down by erosion. Many dinosaurs have to be named on the basis of incomplete skeletons. An incomplete skeleton can be given a name if the scientist thinks it is different enough from all known species. However, sometimes names assigned to two incomplete specimens subsequently turn out to represent the same species of dinosaur. When this happens, the name that was proposed first has priority. Two partial skeletons described by O. C. Marsh were given two names—the first was called *Apatosaurus* in 1877, and the second was named *Brontosaurus* in 1879. When it was discovered many years later that the skeletons represented the same type of animal, one of the names had to be dropped. Because the name *Apatosaurus* was two years older than *Brontosaurus*, the former became the official or correct name. There are many other ways that similar problems develop. A female dinosaur might look very different from a male, and sexually different specimens may be given different species names. Young animals may not resemble the adults, and even the amount of variation between individuals

can make it difficult to recognize how many species are represented by a sample. Sometimes these naming problems can be
resolved by simply studying the specimens more carefully. But
most of the time taxonomic problems can only be resolved by the
discovery of more and better-preserved specimens.

**13. Why do people, especially children, like dinosaurs so
much?** Ever since their initial discovery more than 150 years
ago, dinosaurs have attracted the attention of people of virtually
all ages, backgrounds and cultures. It is well known that children
in particular love dinosaurs. It is also clear that as we learn more
about dinosaurs, they become ever more popular. Why do people
find dinosaurs so interesting? There is no single answer to this
question, even though paleontologists, journalists and even psy-
chologists have studied this phenomenon in detail. Dinosaurs
inspire awe because of the enormous sizes that some of them
reached, and humans in general are fascinated by superlatives—
the longest, the heaviest, the tallest, the most ferocious, and so
on. Dinosaurs are the monsters and dragons of our dreams, except that they really did exist. And there are many mysteries sur-
rounding these animals that we like to wonder about. Why were
dinosaurs so successful that they outcompeted mammals in all of
the higher ecological niches for more than 160 million years?
Why did their populations crash when they seemed to be at the
height of their evolution? What does the extinction of dinosaurs
tell us about our own future as a species?

In recent years, a lot has been learned about dinosaurs, and
our perceptions of what dinosaurs were have gone through some
dramatic changes. We no longer think of dinosaurs as simply
overgrown lizards with small brains, simple behavior and cold
blood. The more we learn about them, the more we marvel at
them. They are the introduction that many people have to the
fascination of science. And in many countries they have become
a cultural phenomenon, the stars of stories, comic strips, ani-
mated cartoons and movies. They not only generate revenues for
everything from museums to movies, but they are heavily used in
advertising to sell products. For many people, dinosaurs are interesting because they are, quite simply, a success story.

14. What is the most popular dinosaur? *Allosaurus, Brachiosaurus, Brontosaurus, Diplodocus, Stegosaurus, Triceratops, Tyrannosaurus* and *Velociraptor* are just a few of the dinosaurs that are frequently cited when people are asked what their favorite dinosaur is. Different types of people may select very different types of dinosaurs as their favorites. Movies, television programs, comic books and other forms of mass entertainment can dramatically affect public familiarity with dinosaur names. However, the dinosaur that appears most frequently in popular books, magazine articles, educational television and movies about dinosaurs is *Tyrannosaurus rex*. As the largest meat-eating animal known to have walked the Earth, with its yard-long jaws and six-inch dagger-like teeth, it is not surprising that most people find this animal awe-inspiring. *Tyrannosaurus* also has the advantage of having a name that has not suffered the changes that have plagued dinosaurs like *Brontosaurus*. It was one of the last of the large, carnivorous dinosaurs. Yet enough mystery still surrounds this animal to make it interesting for scientists when new specimens are discovered.

2. Dinosaur Fossils

15. What is a fossil? Although many definitions of "fossil" (derived from the Latin word for "dug up") have been published, one of the best is that fossils are simply any evidence of extinct life. Bones do not have to be "turned into stone" to be fossils, and usually most of the original bone is present in a dinosaur fossil. Footprints, the impressions left in mud, as well as dung and eggs, are some of the other common types of dinosaur fossils. Although the horny beaks of hadrosaurs (duckbilled dinosaurs), cartilage at the ends of long bones, and skin usually decompose before they have an opportunity to fossilize, these things are sometimes preserved. Most remarkable, perhaps, is the recent discovery that ancient genetic material, including DNA, can be extracted from dinosaur teeth, bones and eggs.

16. How long does it take for a bone to become "fossilized"? Fossilization is a process that can take anything from a few hours to millions of years. "Fossilized" bone is usually considered to be that which has "turned to stone." The process is called permineralization. When a bone becomes buried, groundwater seeps through all of the pores and openings to invade the spaces inside. Minerals carried by the water are deposited inside these spaces, and over time can fill them in completely. This is similar to what happens in the sediments around the bone, where minerals carried in solution are deposited in the spaces to cement sand grains together to form sandstones, silts into siltstones, and so on. The amount of time that it takes for a bone to become completely permineralized is highly variable. If the groundwater is heavily laden with minerals in solution, the process can happen rapidly. Modern bones that fall into mineral springs can become permineralized within a matter of weeks. The preservation of soft tissues in some dinosaurs also suggests that, under exceptional circumstances, fossilization can occur within days. Some of the more common minerals found in permineralized bone are calcite, iron, phosphate and silica. Virtually any mineral that can be carried in solution in water can be found in fossilized bones, however. Dinosaur bones found in northeastern Colorado contain enough uranium to be located by a geiger counter. Dinosaur bones are not always permineralized, however. In Dinosaur Provincial Park in Alberta, dinosaur bones were sometimes encased in ironstone nodules shortly after they were buried 75 million years ago. The nodules prevented water from invading the bones, which for all intents and purposes cannot be distinguished from modern bone. A more spectacular example was found on the North Slope of Alaska, where many thousands of bones lack any significant degree of permineralization. The bones look and feel like old cow bones, and the discoverers of the site did not report it for twenty years because they assumed they were bison, not dinosaur, bones.

17. Has dinosaur skin been found?   In 1909, a remarkable skeleton of the duckbilled dinosaur *Edmontosaurus* was discovered in Wyoming. The specimen, now on display in the American Museum of Natural History in New York, is almost completely encased in its "skin." Since its discovery, fossilized evidence of skin has been found associated with the skeletons of other types of duckbilled dinosaurs (hadrosaurs), plus theropods, sauropods, stegosaurs, ankylosaurs and horned dinosaurs (ceratopsians). The "skin," in most cases, is actually only an impression of the outer surface of the skin. After the animal died, the skin on the lower side of the body pressed into the mud. As the skin decomposed, the impression was left in the mud. When this was filled in by another layer of sand or mud, the skin impression was sometimes preserved. In some cases, these skin impressions are covered by a black film that may represent the carbonized remains of the skin itself. Microscopic examination of fossilized skin from New Mexico revealed both dermal and epidermal layers, showing that the skin itself can be fossilized.

Skin impressions were occasionally left by dinosaurs before they died. There have been several reports of "body impressions," where dinosaurs supposedly lay down in the mud and left their outlines. Unfortunately, none of the reports made so far are convincing. Recently, skin impressions have been found in the bottoms of dinosaur footprints from Alberta and Colorado.

Dinosaur skin was highly variable, not only between different species, but also on different regions of the same body. The skin surfaces of hadrosaurs and tyrannosaurs have a light, pebbly texture that is reminiscent of the hides of thick-skinned mammals like elephants and rhinos. The large Argentinean theropod *Carnotaurus*, *Saurolophus* from Mongolia, and several ceratopsians from Alberta had large "scales" surrounded by mosaics of smaller bumps. Small plates of bone grew within the skin of ankylosaurs and some of the long-necked sauropods. Spinelike frills have been found along the top of a tail of *Edmontosaurus* from Montana, and along the back and tail of *Diplodocus* from Wyoming.

There is a group of South American sauropods called titanosaurids that have bony plates imbedded in their skin, perhaps to provide them with some protection from the attacks of carnivores. The plate-backed stegosaurs have small bony plates in the skin along their necks, backs and sides. This kind of protection is taken to an extreme by the armored ankylosaurs, the backs and sides of which were covered by mosaics of bony plates and spikes imbedded in the skin. Small "osteoderms" (which means "bone in skin") were even found in ankylosaur eyelids, and the skin of the cheeks and throat.

18. Did some dinosaurs have feathers? Since about 1980, a lot of paintings have been done that show small meat-eating dinosaurs with feathers. In some there are just a few long feathers making up crests or frills for adornment. But other paintings show dinosaurs completely covered with feathers. During the 1970s, there was a revolution in the way we think about dinosaurs. Up to that time, they were considered to be cold-blooded animals that were incapable of controlling their body temperatures. But several lines of evidence put this assumption into question, and now most paleontologists are willing to accept the idea that at least some dinosaurs were warm-blooded like mammals and birds. Small theropods (meat-eaters) are considered to be the most likely candidates for warm-bloodedness, in part because of their close relationship with birds. Feathers serve two main functions in birds; they form the major areas of the wings, and they provide insulation to retard heat loss from the body. The evolution of flight would have been a gradual process, and feathers must have been present on the ancestors of birds before they could be adapted into elongate flight feathers. That is, feathers probably first appeared in the small meat-eating dinosaurs that gave rise to birds. They would have been used mostly for insulation, but may also have been used to form display structures, as with modern birds. Although there are good reasons to suspect that small theropods may have been covered by feathers for insulation, skin impressions have never been found with any of the small meat-eating dinosaurs.

19. Has dinosaur DNA been found? The dinosaurs in the book *Jurassic Park* by Michael Crichton were brought back to life because the fictional scientists had found a way to extract DNA (the genetic blueprints of living organisms) from dinosaur blood. The blood was found inside mosquitos trapped in amber (fossilized resin). In reality, only two mosquitos have been found so far in amber, one from Alberta and one from Japan. Fossilized mosquitos are too rare right now to be sacrificed in the hope that they might have dinosaur blood in their digestive systems. However, biting flies are commonly found in Cretaceous amber, and at least one laboratory is actively looking for dinosaur blood in gnats that seem to have specialized in biting very large animals. Even if they succeed in finding dinosaur DNA using this approach, it will be difficult to assess exactly which dinosaur donated the blood. More than a dozen laboratories around the world are actively trying to find dinosaur DNA in dinosaur teeth, bones and eggs. There have been several announcements of success, but the results still need to be confirmed independently by other labs. Assuming that genetic material is recovered from dinosaur fossils, a whole new area of research may open up. The chances of cloning dinosaurs and bringing them back to life seem to be very remote. But understanding the genetic codes of dinosaur species will give paleontologists very powerful tools for determining more precisely the relationships between dinosaurs (including birds).

20. How big are dinosaur eggs? Dinosaur eggs are not as large as most people would think. They have been recovered from many places, including Alberta, Montana and Utah in North America, Argentina, China, France, Mongolia, Romania and South Africa. Considering the enormous sizes that some dinosaurs reached, it is surprising how small dinosaur eggs are. The largest eggs known are less than a foot and a half long, and no more than 8 inches in diameter, which makes them not much larger than ostrich eggs. It is unlikely that any dinosaur ever laid an egg much larger than this anyway. Dinosaur eggs have hard, brittle shells like those of modern birds. The shells are pierced by thousands of tiny pores that allow the exchange of gases between the inside of the egg and the atmosphere outside. Essentially this is so the developing embryos can breathe. As eggs become larger, they become much heavier. The shell needs to be much thicker than that of a small egg; otherwise it would collapse under its own weight. This is because the relationship between the weight of the egg and the strength of the shell increases disproportionately as the egg increases in size. As a simple example, let us assume that we have an egg that is 1" long and compare it with an egg double that length. The larger egg is 2" long, but the surface area has increased by a factor of 2^2. Doubling the length of the egg therefore increases the surface area by a factor of four. However, the weight of the egg is related to its volume, which has increased by a factor of 2^3, or 8. Doubling the length of the egg has increased the weight 8 times, but only quadrupled the surface area. Because the strength of the shell is related to the surface area, the shell has to double in thickness to support the weight. The lower surface-area-to-volume ratio also means that there needs to be four times as many pores to supply the developing embryo with oxygen. An egg four times as long has an even bigger problem, because the surface increases by a factor of 4^2 (16), whereas the weight goes up by 4^3 (64) times. The shell therefore needs to be 4 (64/16) times thicker than that of the one-inch egg, and there needs to be 16 times the number of pores. As an egg becomes progressively bigger, it eventually reaches a point where enough oxygen cannot penetrate the shell to supply the baby growing inside, and where the shell becomes too thick for the embryo to break out anyway. These ratios are what limited the egg size of even dinosaurs that grew to be more than 100 feet long.

21. Can a paleontologist identify which dinosaur species laid which eggs? Since 1923, when fossilized eggs were first identified as being those of dinosaurs, there has been a problem determining which species laid which eggs. Eggs found in Mongolia at that time were assumed to have been laid by *Protoceratops*, which was the most common dinosaur recovered from the rocks where the eggs were found. It took 70 years to discover that at least some of the eggs were laid by the meat-eating dinosaur *Oviraptor*. This dinosaur in fact got its name, which means "egg thief," because of the mistaken identity of the eggs. Rather than stealing the eggs of *Protoceratops*, the *Oviraptor* probably died protecting its own eggs. In spite of all the mistakes made in the early years of studying dinosaur eggs, enough progress has been made so that paleontologists can identify even fragments of eggshell. Most importantly, identifiable embryos have been found within eggs. These include the theropod *Oviraptor* from Mongolia, the hypsilophodont *Orodromeus* from Montana, and the duckbilled dinosaur *Hypacrosaurus* from Alberta. Once eggs have been positively identified by the presence of embryos, that information can be used to identify the same kinds of eggs when embryos are not present. Eggs can be identified by their shapes, their sizes, by the texture of their surfaces or by the patterns with which the eggs are laid in nests. An even better way to identify eggshell is to look at its microscopic, crystalline structure. This is done by cutting very thin slices of the shell, mounting them on slides and looking at them under a light microscope. Scanning electron microscopes can also be used to help determine minute details of structure, which is very different in different groups of dinosaurs.

22. How long did it take for a dinosaur egg to hatch? Scientists have not been able to determine how long it took for a dinosaur egg to hatch. Each species probably took a different length of time, with smaller eggs tending to take less time. Because dinosaurs grew very fast, because they are related to modern birds, and because dinosaur eggs were never much larger than the largest modern bird eggs, the hatching time for ostrich eggs is probably a good indication of how long dinosaur eggs took. This suggests dinosaurs would hatch within six weeks from the day the eggs were laid. From what we have learned about the migration patterns of dinosaurs, this seems to be a reasonable guess.

23. How big was a baby dinosaur when it was born? The maximum size of hatchling dinosaurs would have been controlled largely by the size of the eggs within which they grew. Smaller dinosaurs laid smaller eggs, and therefore the babies would have been smaller when they were born. However, egg size would not have had the same limitations in the smaller dinosaurs. A small dinosaur could have had babies that were about a fifth the size of the adults. The babies of sauropod dinosaurs, on the other hand, were tiny next to the adults. A sauropod that was more than a hundred feet long as an adult would have been only about two feet long at birth, which means that the babies were one fiftieth the size of the adults. These ratios are based on egg size, and on the size relationships between hatchlings and adults in modern lizards, snakes and crocodiles. In a few animals, the ratio can be measured directly. Embryos inside eggs of *Hypacrosaurus stebengeri* were ready to hatch when they died. The babies would have been about 18" long at birth, whereas the adults reached lengths of about 22 feet. The babies of this dinosaur were therefore about one fifteenth the size of the adults. These calculations hold true as long as a dinosaur species was hatched from an egg. It has been suggested that some dinosaurs were born live, just as with mammals and some snakes. Although there is no conclusive evidence to suggest that this happened, if it did the babies would have been larger at birth.

24. How did a dinosaur make its nest and how were the eggs arranged? Like those of modern birds, dinosaur nests were highly variable in appearance. Some dinosaurs appear to have scooped out shallow depressions in the ground, within which they laid their eggs. It has been suggested that vegetation was piled on top of these nests. As the vegetation decomposed, it would produce heat to incubate the eggs. Other dinosaurs (such as *Oviraptor*) seem to have laid their eggs on the surface of the ground, but they scooped sand on top of the eggs to form low mounds.

Although some dinosaurs seem to have laid their eggs one at a time, the majority seem to have laid them in pairs. Sometimes the eggs are stretched out in a line, and sometimes they are clustered together in a round nest. One of the most interesting nest forms is that of small meat-eaters like *Oviraptor*. They appear to have stood on a single spot, but turned as they laid each pair of eggs. The result is a spiral with up to three layers of eggs. The center of the nest, where the dinosaur stood while laying the eggs, is empty except for the sand that was scooped onto the nest as the eggs were being laid.

25. How many eggs were in a dinosaur nest? Dinosaur nests have been discovered with as many as forty eggs in them. It is very rare that nests are found before they have been at least partially destroyed by erosion. Nevertheless, enough complete nests have been found to show that the number of eggs in a nest was as diverse as the dinosaurs that laid them. There seems to have been a tendency for small dinosaurs with relatively large eggs to have laid fewer eggs than large dinosaurs did, and some nests seem to have had as few as two or three eggs in them. Nests with eight to twelve eggs seem to be a common configuration for a variety of small dinosaurs. However, a single, human-sized dinosaur could apparently have laid up to forty eggs in a nest.

26. Did the mother dinosaur remain with the nest until the eggs hatched? Without being able to travel back in time, it is impossible to know whether or not dinosaurs protected their nests. It was once assumed that dinosaurs were primitive animals that must have laid their eggs and abandoned them. However, some remarkable discoveries in Montana since 1979 seem to indicate that duckbilled dinosaurs (hadrosaurs) laid their eggs in huge nesting colonies. Several other sites in the world have now been discovered where numerous nests of the same species of dinosaur were presumably laid in the same area at the same time. One of the few real advantages gained from nesting in colonies is the increased protection of the eggs and the young if the adults remain in the neighborhood. The regular spacing between the nests does seem to be correlated with the size of the adults—the larger the adult dinosaur, the larger the spacing between the nests. The site near Choteau, Montana, provided further evidence that suggested baby dinosaurs remained in their nests for up to several months after they hatched. It is assumed that unless they were being brought food by the adults, the babies would not have survived so long. Because of the behavioral implications, the hadrosaur found at Choteau was given the name *Maiasaura*, which means the "good mother lizard." In China and Mongolia, there are three examples of *Oviraptor* skeletons lying on nests of *Oviraptor* eggs. It seems most likely that the adults were protecting, and possibly incubating, the eggs when they died. However, it is also possible that they died when they were in the process of laying the eggs. Like modern animals, dinosaurs would have practiced a wide range of strategies after the eggs were laid. Some dinosaurs no doubt did walk away from their nests as soon as the eggs were laid. But there is enough evidence to suggest that many species did remain with their eggs until they hatched.

27. What do dinosaur footprints tell us about dinosaurs?

Dinosaur footprints can provide a lot of information about dinosaurs, some of which cannot be deduced from looking at the skeletons. A footprint is made when an animal steps into wet mud or sand to make a natural mold of the foot itself. Under exceptional circumstances, this mold can be so detailed that even the skin is replicated. Because the skin and pads are usually not preserved with dinosaur skeletons, footprints are generally the only evidence to show what the bottom of the foot looked like. Hadrosaur footprints, for example, show that there were large, fleshy pads beneath each of the three toes, and there was another large pad behind the toes, which formed a "heel" mark. In some places, dinosaur bones do not fossilize well, and the only evidence to show that dinosaurs lived there is from the footprints that they left behind. Footprints provide much more evidence if they are found in trackways, because they show what the animals were doing when they were alive. Trackways have shown that dinosaurs walked with their legs underneath their bodies, and that the tails were held above the ground and were never dragged. Mathematical formulas can be used to calculate how fast the dinosaurs that made the trackways were running or walking. Trackway sites can also provide information on the behavior of dinosaurs. Numerous localities now show that plant-eating dinosaurs like sauropods and hadrosaurs often moved in big herds, whereas the meat-eaters moved in smaller, less organized packs.

28.   How big is the largest dinosaur footprint? The smallest?
Dinosaur footprints range in size from less than an inch (2.5 centimeters) to more than 3 feet (one meter). The largest known dinosaur footprints were made by very large sauropod dinosaurs. The footprints of one dinosaur in Morocco are almost four feet (1.15 meters) long, and were made by a sauropod that may have been more than a hundred feet (30 meters) long. An even longer footprint from Korea was given the name *Ultrasaurus*. At the other end of the scale, a footprint found in 22-million-year-old rocks of Nova Scotia is no bigger than a dime. However, it is also possible that this three-toed track may not have been made by a dinosaur.

29.   Can a paleontologist always determine which footprints were made by which dinosaur?   Dinosaur footprints can show a wide range of variation, which makes them potentially identifiable. The tracks of carnivorous dinosaurs usually have narrow toe impressions that end in claw marks, whereas those of herbivores tend to be thicker and rounder. As long as a dinosaur footprint is well preserved, at least the general type of dinosaur that it represents can be identified. Unfortunately, it is almost impossible to identify dinosaur footprints down to the species of animal. There are several reasons for this. First, footprints and bones require different conditions in the environment if they are going to be preserved. Because of this, localities that produce lots of dinosaur bones generally do not produce identifiable footprints, whereas sites with huge concentrations of well-preserved tracks almost always lack dinosaur bones. A more fundamental problem is the fact that foot structure can be very conservative within any major group of dinosaurs. Many different species of hadrosaurs lived at the same time in Dinosaur Provincial Park in Alberta. Because they were all about the same size, it would be impossible to distinguish the tracks of *Brachylophosaurus, Corythosaurus, Edmontosaurus, Gryposaurus, Lambeosaurus, Parasaurolophus* and *Prosaurolophus*. If a person were so lucky as to find footprints leading to a dinosaur that had died in its tracks, then it could be determined who made the trackway. Unfortunately, this has never happened.

Because it is so difficult to associate footprints and skeletons, tracks are usually given their own names. Footprints left by a South American hadrosaur (duckbilled dinosaur) have been named *Hadrosaurichnus*, and those of a large meat-eater from Australia are called *Tyrannosauropus*. The endings "ichnus" and "pus" mean footprint and foot, respectively, and are commonly found in track names.

30. Where are the most dinosaurs found? Where are the best dinosaur museums in the world? There are many dinosaur sites in the world that can be called the richest, depending on how "richness" is defined. In terms of localities that represent single ecosystems, Dinosaur Provincial Park in Alberta and the Nemegt Valley of Mongolia are equally rich. Both have produced hundreds of well-preserved skeletons, and there are at least thirty-five species of dinosaurs at each site. Zigong, in southwestern China, is richest in the sense that it has the most complete skeletons concentrated in an area about the size of a football field. Individual bones of dinosaur skeletons can get all mixed up and deposited in bonebeds, some of which are so rich that they can have more than 100 bones per cubic yard. To determine which site was richest in this sense, however, one would have to decide how big an area this should be averaged over. In most cases, it makes more sense to just talk about the areas that consistently stimulate the greatest amount of research on dinosaurs. Using this criterion, the richest areas are undoubtedly the western interior basin of North America (including Alberta, Colorado, the Dakotas, Montana, Saskatchewan, Utah and Wyoming), the Gobi Desert of China and Mongolia and Patagonia (in Argentina).

There are many good dinosaur museums around the world, and each has its individual strengths. The American Museum of Natural History in New York City has one of the strongest collections of dinosaurs from the United States, Canada, Mongolia and many other countries. The dinosaur galleries have recently been renovated and are more exciting than ever. One of the largest exhibitions of dinosaurs is at the Royal Tyrrell Museum of Palaeontology in the badlands outside of Drumheller, Alberta. Here visitors can see everything from fossils being excavated outside the museum to more than 50 dinosaur skeletons on display. If one ever has the opportunity to go to Moscow, the finest display of dinosaurs from the Gobi Desert is in the Orlov Museum of Paleontology. By area, the largest dinosaur exhibition is the Zigong Dinosaur Museum in the province of Sichuan in China. Like Dinosaur National Monument in Utah, the building has been constructed over an enormous bonebed.

31. Have any frozen dinosaurs been found in the Arctic?
Dinosaur fossils have been found in Alaska, the Northwest Territories, the Yukon, Greenland, Siberia and the island of Spitzbergen. Although these fossils had to be removed from frozen ground, there was no permafrost when dinosaurs lived in these lands. The Greenland and Spitzbergen dinosaurs actually lived at more southern latitudes, but their fossils were carried north by continental drift. The dinosaurs from the other sites actually did live in the Arctic during the Cretaceous period (between 145 and 65 million years ago). At that time, however, there was no permanent ice cap, and the dinosaurs would have prospered because there was so much to eat during the summer months when plant growth was stimulated by 24 hours of daily sunlight. During the winter months, the dinosaurs had the choice of either migrating south or hibernating.

3. Interesting Facts

32. Did all dinosaurs live at the same time? All dinosaurs did not live at the same time, nor did any species have a worldwide distribution. Dinosaurs dominated the environments on land from 225 million years ago until 65 million years ago. Over their 160-million-year reign, they were constantly changing and adapting. Because of the incompleteness of the fossil record, it is difficult to determine how long an individual species survived. However, it seems as if no species lasted for longer than 5 million years, and most would have been around for less than 2 million. Dinosaur species are therefore characteristic of particular periods of time. *Diplodocus*, which lived about 150 million years ago, could never have been hunted by a *Tyrannosaurus*, an animal that did not appear until more than 80 million years later.

33. What is the biggest dinosaur? The longest dinosaur presently known is *Seismosaurus*, which has an estimated length of between 114 and 150 feet (35–45 meters). Unfortunately, the whole skeleton of this animal was not recovered from its site in New Mexico. Enough of the specimen was excavated to show that the tail was considerably longer than those of its nearest relatives, *Apatosaurus* and *Diplodocus*. It appears to have been a rather slender sauropod, and its estimated weight is less than 30 tons.

Like the longest dinosaur, the tallest dinosaur was also a sauropod. A fragmentary animal from the Dry Mesa Quarry in Colorado is closely related to the well-known *Brachiosaurus*, but appears to have been slightly longer. This animal was first called *Ultrasaurus*, although that name had been used previously for a dinosaur footprint from Korea. Consequently, it has been renamed *Ultrasauros*. This animal had a long neck with neck vertebrae as much as five feet (1.5 meters) long, and its front limbs were longer than its hind limbs. The head could be lifted as much as

40 feet (12 meters) above the ground. This has puzzled scientists, because a normal heart and circulatory system would be incapable of pumping blood that high off the ground. It has been proposed that there were additional pumps along the arteries in the neck, but there is no way that this can be proven at this time.

Sauropods were unquestionably the heaviest dinosaurs, and there are several types that are contenders for being the heaviest animals that ever lived on land. In fact, the weight estimates of a new type of sauropod in Argentina range as high as 100 tons, which puts it in the same category as the largest whales. *Argentinosaurus* has only been partially excavated at this time, but the size of the limb bones and vertebrae indicate that this was a very massive animal.

34. What is the smallest dinosaur?   Some very small dinosaurs have been found in recent years, one of which received the name *Mussasaurus* ("Mouse lizard"). This animal is so small that a whole skeleton fits in the palms of an adult human's hands. Other dinosaurs have been discovered that are about the same size. However, all of these tiny specimens are either embryos or newly hatched individuals, and the adults would have been much larger. At present, the smallest adult dinosaur is *Compsognathus*. This small carnivorous dinosaur is about the size of a chicken, and would have weighed no more than five pounds.

35. What is the largest meat-eater?   The largest predator presently known to have lived on land is *Tyrannosaurus rex*, a dinosaur first discovered more than 90 years ago in Montana and Wyoming. In recent years, many new and more complete specimens have been discovered in western North America, the largest of which is 45 feet (13 meters) long with an estimated weight of more than six tons. This was not the only giant meat-eater, however. During the Jurassic period, both *Torvosaurus* and a close relative of *Allosaurus* (*Eupanterius*) were almost as big. *Acrocanthosaurus*, from hundred-million-year-old rocks of Oklahoma and Texas, was also close to *Tyrannosaurus* in size. In 1994, a new type of meat-eater was discovered in Argentina. *Giganotosaurus* had a skull that was longer than that of *Tyrannosaurus rex*.

However, its body and tail were actually slightly shorter, so the total length of the animal was only 42 feet (12.7 meters). Another theropod, probably *Cacharodontosaurus*, from Morocco, also appears to have been as large or larger than *Tyrannosaurus rex*.

36. Which dinosaur was the smartest? *Troodon* had the largest relative brain size of any known dinosaur. It is difficult to evaluate the relative intelligence of living animals, let alone extinct animals. Relative brain size is one way that the intelligence of an animal can be estimated. Although the brain itself does not fossilize, it is almost completely surrounded by bone in most animals with backbones. The bones that surround the brain are called the braincase, and the cavity inside usually follows the contours of the outer surface of the brain itself. A replica of the brain of a fossilized animal can therefore be obtained by pouring liquid rubber or some other flexible casting compound into the cleaned-out cavity of a braincase. This not only shows the shapes and sizes of the different lobes of the brain, but also indicates where the nerves split off from the brain itself. Brain size varies considerably with the size of an animal. An example of how relative brain size changes can be seen in humans. The heads of babies are large mostly because of the relatively large size of the brain. As a person grows up, the body grows in volume, weight and length faster than the brain does. Therefore an adult human has a head (and brain) which looks smaller in relation to the body than it did when that person was a baby. These scaling effects are also evident between big animals and small animals. Mathematical formulas comparing brain weight and body weight have been worked out to determine how big brains really are if the scaling effects are taken into account. Although most dinosaurs had brains that seem ridiculously small for their body sizes, the majority have relative brain sizes that are comparable to those of modern crocodiles. Sauropods have brains that are much smaller than the norm, whereas some of the meat-eating dinosaurs have brains that are considerably larger than those of crocodiles. The largest-brained theropods include *Troodon*, from the Cretaceous of North America. This man-sized dinosaur had a brain that was six times the size of the brain of a crocodile of the same body weight. In fact, the brain of this dinosaur was as big'as, or bigger than, the brain of any of the mammals and birds that were its contemporaries!

37. Which dinosaur was the stupidest? If one assumes that brain size is correlated with intelligence, then sauropods were probably the stupidest animals of all times. These gigantic animals, which might have weighed as much as 100 tons, had brains that never weighed more than a few pounds. In comparison with a crocodile, the relative size of a sauropod brain was only about a quarter of the size. But this is an indication of the problem in using relative brain size as an indication of intelligence. Trackway and bonebed evidence show that sauropod dinosaurs were capable of the complicated behavior that is normally equated with intelligence. For example, they moved in structured herds in which the young were kept toward the center of the group where they could be protected from carnivores. And it is hard to dispute the success of sauropods, which survived for more than 120 million years even though they had small heads.

38. Which was the fastest dinosaur? It is impossible to determine how fast any particular dinosaur ran without going back in time with a stopwatch to make observations. Because we cannot do that, scientists have come up with several ways to estimate how fast dinosaurs may have run. The lengths of the legs, the proportions of the various leg bones, the length of the body, the estimated body weight and many other factors can be compared with living animals. Calculations provide evidence of the speeds some of these dinosaurs might have reached. For example, *Struthiomimus* had similar body proportions and size to a modern ostrich, an animal that can run up to 50 miles (80 kilometers) per hour.

Trackways provide more direct evidence on how fast dinosaurs moved. When any animal runs, the distance between footprints increases as speed increases. The trackways of modern animals whose running speeds were known were measured by one scientist. Thousands of these measurements were used to develop a mathematical formula to calculate how fast an animal was moving by measuring its footprint length and the distance between individual tracks. This formula was then applied to dinosaur trackways. The fastest-moving dinosaur so far recorded was a small, man-sized meat-eater whose trackway was found in Texas. The calculations suggest that this animal was moving about 25 miles (40 km) per hour when it left its trackway. Although this is not particularly fast, it is doubtful that the animal was moving across the slippery mud at its top speed.

Using two methods of speed analysis, it is quite clear that the fastest dinosaurs were the theropods. Among known meat-eaters, the ornithomimids, which include *Gallimimus*, *Ornithomimus* and *Struthiomimus*, were the best adapted for running at high speeds.

4. Dinosaurian Biology

39. How long would a dinosaur live? Because of the huge size of many dinosaurs, and because some tortoises can live to be hundreds of years old, it is often assumed that dinosaurs lived to ripe old ages. Comparison with living animals of all kinds suggests that the largest dinosaurs probably had long life-spans. Quite simply, it would take many years for an animal to grow as large as *Brachiosaurus* or *Tyrannosaurus*, and it would not make any biological sense to put so much effort into growth unless the large animals had long lives. Recently, studies of the microscopic structure of bones and teeth have revealed daily growth lines that can be counted. This research suggests that some of the man-sized theropods lived to be fifteen or twenty years of age. Unfortunately, the bones of larger animals underwent drastic structural changes as they grew. As bone was added to the outside of a growing leg bone, it was resorbed (dissolved) from the middle of the same bone. This is not surprising considering that adult dinosaur bones could be more than 25 times the length of the baby bones, and that the whole skeleton of a baby could fit inside the marrow cavity of a single adult limb bone. It is safe to suggest that the largest dinosaurs lived to be more than 50 years old, and it is possible that some of them lived hundreds of years.

40. How do we know what color dinosaurs were? Nobody knows what color dinosaurs were during Mesozoic times. Like their closest relatives (birds, crocodiles), dinosaurs generally would have been most active during daylight hours. Study of the eyes and brains of dinosaurs suggests that these animals relied heavily on the sense of sight, and like birds they were probably able to see in color. The frills, horns and crests of dinosaurs show that they relied on visual clues to identify potential mates and rivals, and color would have been a suitable way to accentuate these characteristics. Patterns in the skin are even suggestive of color patterning.

So far, no method has been worked out to determine what color a dinosaur was. Like modern animals, they probably went through the whole spectrum of possibilities. It is possible for colors to be preserved in fossils, however. A fifty-million-year-old soft-shelled turtle from New Mexico has its colors preserved on the shell (red with black dots). And there are examples of two-hundred-million-year-old sea shells that still have color patterns on them. Although these are extremely rare fossils, they do show that it may be possible to determine the actual colors of some dinosaurs. Chemical traces in the skin and DNA analysis offer other potential ways of determining their colors. Although these seem like very remote possibilities at this time, many things being done in paleontological studies seemed impossible twenty years ago.

41. Were dinosaurs warm-blooded? The idea that dinosaurs might have been warm-blooded animals like birds and mammals is not a new idea. It first appeared almost five decades ago. During the 1970s, there was a steady increase in evidence suggesting that dinosaurs were more mammal-like in their physiology than they were like living reptiles. This radical change in how most people viewed dinosaurs triggered a renaissance in research and public interest that is still going on today. The many lines of evidence that suggest warm-bloodedness in dinosaurs include their relationship to birds, their high growth rates, their ability to compete with mammals, their upright postures, the activity levels indicated by trackways, their preference for high latitudes and the development of anatomical structures that allowed them to breathe more efficiently. Although there are many reasons to believe that dinosaurs may have been warm-blooded, at present there is no way to show conclusively that they were warm-blooded. The majority of paleontologists who work with dinosaurs feel that small therapods like *Deinonychus*, *Velociraptor* and *Troodon* were probably warm-blooded, but that most other dinosaurs were not. A few believe that all dinosaurs had active, mammal-like metabolic rates.

Birds and mammals are endotherms that control their own body temperatures by internal mechanisms, whereas cold-blooded

animals (ectotherms) need external stimuli like the sun to warm
or cool their bodies. Living systems tend to be more complex than
people generally give them credit for. Examination of modern
animals reveals that warm-bloodedness has been acquired many
times independently. Birds and mammals are not closely related
to each other, and both had cold-blooded ancestors. Some spiders, some sharks and tuna are warm-blooded, and among extinct
animals flying reptiles (pterosaurs) were almost certainly endotherms. On the other hand, some birds have no control of their
body temperatures when they are born, and some modern mammals (such as tree sloths) are effectively cold-blooded. There is
some evidence to suggest that dinosaurs may have been warm-
blooded as babies, but switched to cold-bloodedness as they
matured. Warm-bloodedness would have allowed the young animals to grow rapidly, whereas cold-bloodedness is a more efficient
system that would have substantially reduced the amount of food
that an adult had to eat.

42. Why did *Tyrannosaurus rex* have such small arms? In
comparison with total body size, the arms of *Tyrannosaurus rex*
and its relatives are ridiculously small. Although the hands were
incapable of reaching the mouth, close examination of the arms
suggests that they were not useless appendages. The claws are
huge, and curve to end in sharp points. The upper arm bones are
comparable in size to those of adult humans, but are much thicker
and stronger. Muscle attachments on the bones show that the
muscles were large and powerful. In fact, analysis of the athletic
ability of a *Tyrannosaurus* arm suggests that it would have been
capable of lifting almost half a ton! Tyrannosaurid arm bones
often show evidence of healed fractures and other injuries. This
would not be expected if the arms were not being used.

Why were the arms so short then? Tyrannosaurids and other
meat-eating dinosaurs were like walking teeter-totters—the tail
balanced the front of the body, and the hips and hind legs formed
the fulcrum. As theropods increased in size, the skull became
disproportionately large and heavy. Consider the fact that the crown
and root of a *Tyrannosaurus* tooth could be more than a foot long.
There were more than fifty of these heavy teeth in every skull! To

keep the front of the body as light as possible, tyrannosaurids had many special adaptations for reducing weight. Skull bones were full of sinuses filled by air from openings in the nose and throat, and vertebrae and ribs were filled by air acquired by extensions of the lungs. The front of the body was shortened by introducing more curvature into the neck and by reducing the lengths of the individual vertebrae. The only function of the arms was to hold the prey long enough for the terrible teeth and jaws of the tyrannosaur to do their job. The arms could therefore be reduced in length and weight without affecting their function. It is therefore likely that the arms of *Tyrannosaurus* became short to lighten up the front of the body.

43.   Was *Tyrannosaurus rex* a scavenger or a predator?
Like most carnivorous animals, *Tyrannosaurus rex* was probably both a hunter and a scavenger. It was such an enormous animal that many scientists believe that it could not have been an active hunter. It is almost a moot point because most predators are opportunists, becoming scavengers when dead meat is available. And animals that are traditionally thought of as scavengers are also active hunters. The most highly adapted mammalian scavenger is the hyena. Its powerful jaws allow it to consume both the flesh and bones of carcasses, but its stocky body does not give the impression that it could run down any prey. Nevertheless, a hyena hunts and kills about 30% of what it eats.

There is evidence in Dinosaur Provincial Park (Alberta) of a mass drowning of a herd of horned dinosaurs, and there is no doubt that tyrannosaurs scavenged the carcasses when they washed ashore. But this was an exceptional, short-term event, and the tyrannosaurs would probably have starved to death if they had had to wait for other animals to die.

Tyrannosaurus, in spite of its large size, had longer legs and a lighter build than the hadrosaurs and ceratopsians that were undoubtedly its source of food. There would be little sense for an animal to be adapted for speed if it was only chasing dead animals.

44.   How could sauropods support their enormous weights on land?   At one time it was believed by many scientists that

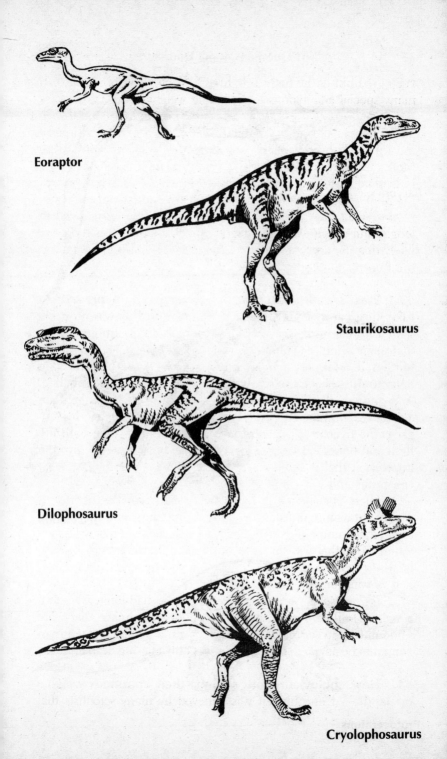

Eoraptor

Staurikosaurus

Dilophosaurus

Cryolophosaurus

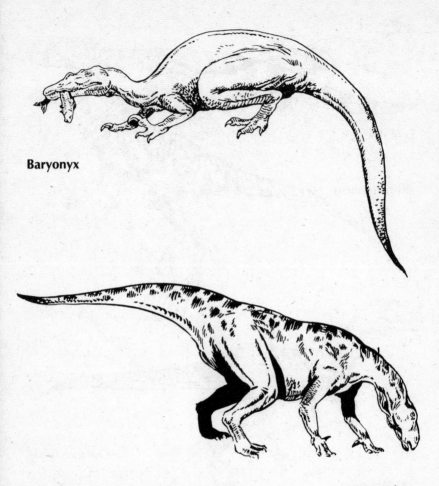

Baryonyx

Iguanodon

Protoceratops

Psittacosaurus

Ouranosaurus

Anatotitan

Centrosaurus

Velociraptor

Edmontosaurus

Euoplocephalus

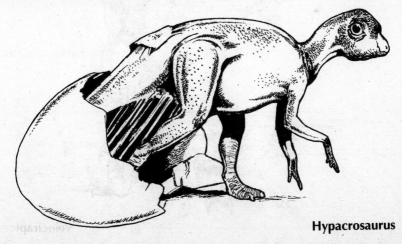

Hypacrosaurus

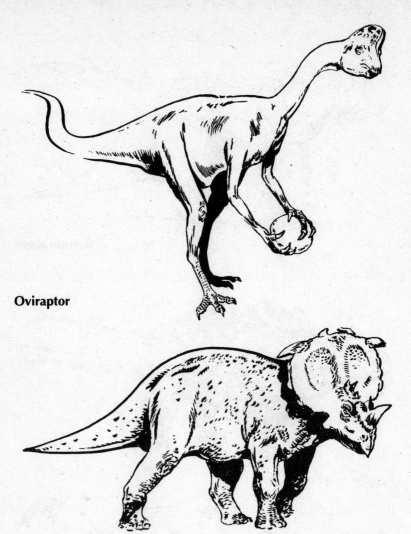

Oviraptor

Pachyrhinosaurus

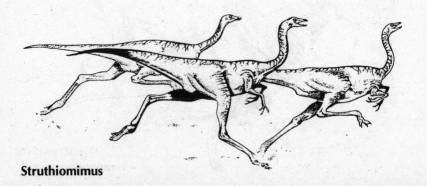

Struthiomimus

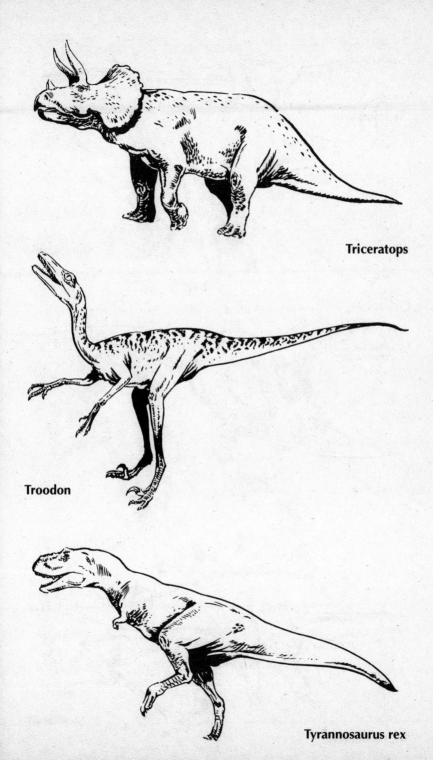

Triceratops

Troodon

Tyrannosaurus rex

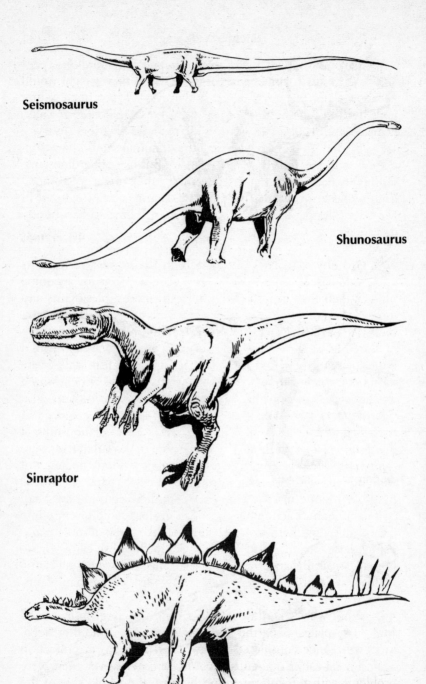

Seismosaurus

Shunosaurus

Sinraptor

Stegosaurus

long-necked sauropods like *Diplodocus* and *Brachiosaurus* spent all of their time in large bodies of water where their weight would be buoyed up. However, closer study revealed that many sauropods lived in regions where there were no large bodies of water. Fossil footprints also show that these giants walked on land.

It is hard to conceive of how these animals could have supported up to 100 tons of weight on land. But like other dinosaurs, sauropods held their legs directly under their bodies. Sauropod limb bones are very massive, and their joints were structured in ways that large mammals like elephants have subsequently developed.

45. Did any dinosaurs live mainly in the water? Dinosaurs were land-based animals, and none were adapted for spending most of their lives in water the way ichthyosaurs, plesiosaurs and mosasaurs were. Even so, all dinosaurs were probably strong swimmers, and at least two types of meat-eating dinosaurs may have preferred to catch and eat fish. *Baryonyx* is a large animal with a long, low, crocodile-like skull. Partially digested fish scales were found in the stomach region of the one and only specimen, which was discovered in England. Several species of therizinosaurs (also referred to as segnosaurs) have only recently been recognized in Asia. Scientists were initially puzzled about the relationships of these strange animals, but were finally able to show that they were theropods. These animals generally had low, stout bodies, but were armed with large, strongly recurved claws. Most specimens have been found in lake deposits, where they seem to have been quite abundant. Each tooth is leaf-like in shape, and has multiple cusps. Although therizinosaur teeth look like those of some plant-eating dinosaurs, they also resemble the teeth of fish-eating mammals like seals. Because their immediate ancestors were flesh-eating animals, it seems more likely that they ate fish rather than plants.

46. What were the plates on the back of a *Stegosaurus* used for? The plates along the back of *Stegosaurus* and other stegosaurs were once considered to have been a means of protection against meat-eating dinosaurs like *Allosaurus*. However, there were problems with this interpretation because the whole side of the animal was unprotected, and the plates were thin enough that large theropods could have bitten right through them. The plates may have provided some protection, but that was clearly not their main purpose.

The surface of a stegosaur plate is covered by canals for blood vessels. The presence of blood vessels on the outside suggests that the plates served alternatively as radiators and solar collectors. If a stegosaur was cold, it would orient its body so that the sun was shining directly on the plates, so that the blood would pick up and carry the heat into the rest of the body. A hot stegosaur, on the other hand, could move into the shade where it would turn so that even the slightest breeze removed heat from the blood vessels in the skin overlying the plates. The plates, which also seem to have been disproportionately small in young animals, might also have helped the adults to recognize potential mates or rivals.

Toward the ends of their tails, all stegosaurs had numerous pairs of spikes. These were probably used to ward off overaggressive theropods. Recently, it has also been discovered that most stegosaurs had a long spike over each shoulder as well.

47. Were any dinosaurs poisonous? Poison glands are never fossilized, so it is impossible to determine whether or not some dinosaurs were poisonous. One of the new Hollywood myths created by the movie *Jurassic Park* is that some dinosaurs, like *Dilophosaurus*, could spit poison. The idea was proposed as a way of explaining a gap between the front and back teeth in the upper jaw of *Dilophosaurus*. Although this gap could potentially have housed a poison gland, the idea cannot be either proved or disproved.

48. Can we see differences between male and female dinosaurs? Like many species of modern animals, including the dinosaurian derivatives that we call birds, males and females of dinosaur species did not always look the same. Such differences are not easy to interpret, especially if only a few specimens are known for any single species. There are many examples where the males and females look different enough from each other that initially paleontologists considered them to be distinct species.

These mistakes were sorted out when enough specimens (especially those of young animals) were discovered to show growth trends. Usually there are no significant differences in physical appearances between males and females until they are almost mature. The hadrosaur *Hypacrosaurus* can serve as a good example. These animals had very low crests or bumps on top of the head when they hatched from the eggs. The crest remained low in both males and females until individuals reached about two thirds of their adult size. The crest then started to develop rapidly, but because it was growing more rapidly in what we are assuming to be the males, the males soon had relatively larger crests than the females.

There are many specimens of two relatively primitive small theropods known as *Coelophysis* and *Syntarsus*. Among the adult specimens there are individuals that are relatively lightly built, and others that are larger and more robust. Because there are approximately the same number of each type, it is believed that these are sexual differences.

In *Tyrannosaurus rex*, there is some evidence to suggest that the largest, most massive individuals were female. Because the female needs a wider pelvic canal to lay eggs, the hips are wider. Furthermore, there are some differences at the base of the tail. The blood vessels and nerves that run along the bottom of the tail are protected by a series of small bones called chevrons or haemal arches. The chevrons start farther back on a female's tail, again so there is more room for the egg to come out. This pattern, which is also known to exist in *Troodon* and its relatives, can still be found in egg-laying crocodiles and lizards.

Dinosaurs with crests, horns and frills almost invariably show differences between the males and females. In hooded hadrosaurs, the crests are larger and showier in the supposed males. Horned dinosaurs like *Triceratops* seem to have sexual differences in the curvatures of the large horns over the eyes. Another ceratopsian known as *Pachyrhinosaurus* has replaced the bony horns on its face with a massive boss of bone over the nose, and a smaller lump of bone over each eye. In one of the sexes, presumably the male, the bony boss is domed on top, whereas that of the female seems to be dished out, which makes it much lighter. In addition to this, the male has small, extra horns rising out of the middle of the crest over the neck, and huge, forward curving horns on the back of the frill.

As dinosaur species become better known, it is inevitable that more sexual differences are going to be discovered.

49. Did dinosaurs have diseases and other problems with their health? Dinosaurs would have had health problems, just as modern animals of all types do. Most diseases and injuries in modern animals do not leave any scars on the bones. This would also have been true for extinct animals, and therefore it is not surprising that our understanding of dinosaurian diseases is quite limited.

Most dinosaur skeletons seem to have rehealed bone injuries, ranging from broken fingers, toes and ribs to broken leg bones that must have been very painful to the living animals. One hadrosaur had a broken jaw that caused some messy problems in the growing teeth, but the animal obviously survived for a long time after it had the injury. Injuries at the backs of young horned-dinosaur skulls could cause the neck crests to grow in strange, asymmetrical ways. Shallow wounds sometimes got infected, and abscesses would invade the adjacent bones to leave great gaping holes. There are several specimens of plant-eaters that appear to have been attacked and bitten to the bone by carnivores, but escaped and lived long enough for the bones to heal. Some dinosaurs had arthritis in their joints, and bone cancer has also been reported.

5. Feeding

50. Were all dinosaurs ferocious? The world dinosaurs lived in was probably no more violent than that of any modern natural ecosystem populated by large animals. Most dinosaurs were plant-eaters, and the meat-eaters made up less than ten percent of any dinosaur fauna. The plant-eaters were probably shy animals that would generally flee when approached, although some of them may have been aggressive when they were protecting their young. Like lions on the modern African veldt, the theropods only would have been dangerous when they were hungry. The rest of the time they probably rested peacefully.

51. How can you tell what a dinosaur ate? The easiest way to determine what any extinct animal ate is to look at its teeth. Carnivorous animals have relatively simple, cone-like teeth that are good for biting into the flesh of other animals. The presence of serrations along the front and back edges of a theropod tooth helped the carnivore slice the meat into pieces small enough to swallow. The teeth of primitive dinosaurian herbivores (plant-eaters) were leaf-shaped with multiple cusps for chopping up plants. The most advanced plant-eating dinosaurs were the hadrosaurs and ceratopsians, which both had very sophisticated batteries of teeth for slicing and grinding leaves and twigs into small pieces before they were swallowed. In the dental batteries, the spaces between individual teeth disappeared so that the teeth formed a continuous grinding surface. Because teeth are worn down quickly by eating plants, hadrosaurs had as many as four new teeth growing up from below to replace any tooth that was in use.

The life habits of dinosaurs can also be determined by looking at other parts of the skeletons. The claws of carnivores are usually strongly curved and taper to sharp points, whereas those of herbivores tend to be broad, flat and hoof-like.

Analysis of the chemistry of bones can sometimes give clues as to whether an animal is a herbivore or a carnivore. Multiple forms, or isotopes, exist for elements like oxygen, nitrogen and carbon, but only one form is stable for each. The ratios of different isotopes of the same element have remained relatively constant in the atmosphere over time. However, the isotopic composition of an element in plants is altered when animals eat the plants and incorporate the element into their bodies. The ratio is further altered when carnivorous animals eat the plant-eaters. By measuring the isotopic ratios in fossilized bones, paleontologists can sometimes determine whether an animal was a herbivore or a carnivore.

52. How much food would a dinosaur eat in a day? It is almost impossible to determine at this time how much food any one species of dinosaur ate in a single day. We know that in living mammals, a single shrew will eat a negligible amount of food, whereas an elephant will consume up to 330 pounds (150 kilograms) of food daily. If we look at it from the perspective of how much an animal eats in relation to its body weight, we end up with a very different picture The daily food intake of a shrew amounts to its body weight, whereas the food eaten by an elephant represents less than 5% of its body weight. This relationship would have been true for dinosaurs as well—the larger a dinosaur became, the less food it had to eat in relation to its total body weight. Although this is well understood, food intake also depends on many other factors. Animals eating high-quality food like nuts and seeds do not need to eat as much as animals that consume leaves, twigs and other low-quality food. Warm-blooded animals must eat a lot more food than cold-blooded animals in order to maintain their high body temperatures. It still has not been unequivocally shown whether dinosaurs were either cold- or warm-blooded, but if they were the latter their food intake could have been 400% higher.

53. How could *Apatosaurus (Brontosaurus)*, *Brachiosaurus*, *Diplodocus* and other sauropods eat enough to stay alive when they had such small heads? Sauropods have such small heads that it seems impossible for them to have eaten enough food to stay alive. However, things are not always what they seem to be at first appearance. No animal takes in an appreciably greater amount of food in a mouthful than it can swallow, but the mouth is often much bigger than the throat because it also contains whatever extra equipment is needed to process the food. Some animals do a lot of food processing before they swallow the food. Hadrosaurs, ceratopsians, elephants, horses and cows all have relatively large heads because of their sophisticated mechanisms for preparing food so that it can be digested more easily once it reaches the stomach. Sauropods had to develop a different strategy, however, because of the long necks that allowed them to reach high into the trees for food. Such long necks never would have evolved if there had not been adaptations to lighten the weight of the head and neck. Sauropod heads became small by keeping their functions as simple as possible. Even the small size of the brain may be linked to weight reduction. Although these animals had teeth, they were very simple in structure and functioned only to strip off leaves and twigs that were swallowed without chewing. The plant material was processed in the stone-filled muscular sac within the body cavity, similar to the "crop" of modern birds like the pigeon. Basically, the head of a sauropod is not much more than an extension of the throat, and there was no need for it to be any bigger than it was. Sauropods may also have reduced their volume of food intake by selectively eating only high-quality foods.

54. How big a bite could a *Tyrannosaurus rex* take? The jaws of *Tyrannosaurus rex* were close to five feet (1.5 meters) long, and could probably open as wide as three feet (1 meter). The teeth and jaws were extremely powerful, and were adapted to biting right through both flesh and bone. Occasionally, skeletons of hadrosaurs and ceratopsians are found that were eaten by tyrannosaurs. Smaller bones seem to have been bitten off and swallowed. Larger, thicker bones often show signs of parallel tooth marks left as the jaws bit off the meat. Each bite would have removed several hundred pounds of flesh from the prey. Given the opportunity, it would only have been necessary for *Tyrannosaurus* to bite a man once.

55. Did dinosaurs have baby teeth like humans, cats and dogs? Like mammals, dinosaurs replaced their old teeth with new teeth. However, mammals have only two sets of teeth. When the baby teeth are lost, the second, replacement set of teeth stays with a mammal for the rest of its life. If a second tooth is broken, worn down or decayed, it cannot be fixed or replaced in any natural way. But dinosaurs (and in fact most other nonmammalian animals that have teeth) replaced their teeth at regular intervals of time with new teeth. Comparison of the daily growth lines in the teeth of dinosaurs with those of modern crocodiles suggests that a tooth in the mouth of a meat-eating dinosaur was only in active use for 1.5 to two years, after which it fell out and was replaced by a new one. The rates of replacement were probably much higher in plant-eating dinosaurs, although these have not been studied by scientists yet.

Because we do not know how long most species of dinosaurs lived, we cannot be sure how many complete sets of teeth most would have had in a lifetime. Small meat-eating dinosaurs would have had at least ten sets, and the largest dinosaurs might have had at least five times that number. Teeth were replaced in very specific sequences. Two adjacent teeth were never replaced at the same time, because that would have left too big a gap in the jaw.

56. What happened if a dinosaur broke a tooth? Did dinosaurs have cavities in their teeth? Teeth were replaced by new teeth in any species of dinosaur at a regular rate. When a dinosaur's tooth broke, the unbroken part would stay in the jaw until it was its turn to be replaced. But eventually a new tooth would fill the gap left by the broken tooth. Dinosaur teeth were very tough, and it would take a lot to break them. In meat-eating dinosaurs, breakage was most likely to occur when the animal bit into the bones of other animals. Usually the teeth did not break off completely. However, fossilized theropod teeth often have chips of enamel spalled off from the tip or the edges.

A flying-reptile skeleton found in Dinosaur Park in 1992 has many tooth marks on its bones, showing that it had been eaten by a theropod. In this case, the theropod was identified as *Velociraptor,* because one of its teeth had broken off and stuck in one of the bones. Several hadrosaur tail vertebrae found in Montana also have the broken tips of tyrannosaur teeth imbedded in them.

Dinosaurs replaced their teeth throughout their life, so they did not have to worry about tooth decay. There are a few documented examples of hadrosaurs with jaw infections that caused decay in some of the teeth, but this is not really the same problem that humans have with cavities.

57. Which dinosaur had the most teeth? Duckbilled dinosaurs (hadrosaurs) had the most teeth known for any dinosaur. The teeth were packed closely together, and there were as many as four replacement teeth growing up from below each tooth that was in active use. As a hadrosaur grew up and its jaws got longer, it would add new tooth positions. Therefore the adults had many more teeth than the babies did. In a big noncrested hadrosaur like *Edmontosaurus*, there were as many as 60 functional teeth in each quadrant of the mouth (right upper jaw, left upper jaw, right and left lower jaws), for a total of 240 active teeth. Below each tooth, however, there were another 3 or 4 replacement teeth. Therefore this dinosaur had more than 1,000 teeth present in its skull when it was mature. Some other hadrosaurs, like *Shantungosaurus* from China, may have had even more teeth because they were bigger animals. However, their teeth have not been counted.

58. Which dinosaur had the largest teeth? The longest teeth presently known for any dinosaur are those of *Tyrannosaurus rex*. The crown of the largest tooth of the upper jaw can be seven inches (18 cm) in length, and if the root is included, the complete tooth is more than a foot (30 cm) long. *Tyrannosaurus* was a very large animal, so it is not surprising that it had large teeth. However, the teeth are also disproportionately long, and are relatively longer than those of its closest relatives (*Albertosaurus, Alioramus, Daspletosaurus, Nanotyrannus* and *Tarbosaurus*).

59. Why did some dinosaurs swallow stones? Animals swallow stones for several different reasons. In crocodiles, walruses, plesiosaurs and many aquatic animals, stones are swallowed as ballast. They are housed within the stomach, but do not help to process food. The stones simply make the animal heavier to help it stay underwater. They sit low in the body to help stabilize the body, which otherwise would have a tendency to roll over.

Pigeons and other seed-eating birds swallow stones for a very different reason. Because these birds do not have teeth for grinding up their food, they swallow stones to fulfill this function. The stones end up in a muscular expansion of the digestive tract called a gizzard. Here the stones and seeds are ground together. Because the stones are much harder, the seeds are broken into smaller pieces that can be digested more easily. Only small pieces of the stones break off and continue down the digestive tract with the food. Gizzard stones become rounded, highly polished and smooth. Sauropod dinosaurs used much the same system in that massive numbers of stones were swallowed to grind up, in a muscular sac along the digestive tract, the leaves and twigs that they swallowed. These masses of stone are sometimes found within the rib cages of sauropod skeletons, but more frequently the highly polished stones (called gastroliths) are found isolated in the fossil-bearing rocks. The only nonsauropod dinosaur presently known to have used gizzard stones is *Psittacosaurus*. Hadrosaurs, ceratopsians and most other plant-eating dinosaurs used their teeth to grind up their food, and therefore did not use gastroliths to do this job.

60. Could a hadrosaur "chew its cud" like a cow? Hadrosaurs would have eaten types of food similar to that eaten by deer, elephants and other large, modern herbivores, but it is unlikely that they processed food in the same way. Large plant-eating animals are usually not selective feeders; that is, they are too big to select and eat the small but most nutritious parts of a plant (fruit, nuts, seeds). Instead, they tend to eat leaves and twigs, which have a relatively low food value and are difficult to digest. Large herbivores like cattle, elephants, ankylosaurs, ceratopsians and hadrosaurs must eat huge quantities of food, which must be held in the digestive system for a relatively long time. Microorganisms in the gut help break down the cellulose into more digestible starches and sugars. Cattle, deer and other modern ruminants help the process along by rechewing the partially digested food (cud). There is no way to determine if dinosaurs did this too, but it is such a specialized type of behavior that it seems unlikely that it evolved independently in such different animals. Nevertheless, the wide, well-rounded bodies of herbivorous dinosaurs indicate that they did have huge guts within which the low-quality food that they were eating was processed by digestive acids and microorganisms.

6. Dinosaur Senses

61. Did dinosaurs hear well? Without performing hearing tests, it is difficult to know how well any dinosaur could hear. However, the tiny ear bone (stapes) has been found with a wide range of dinosaur skeletons. The inner ear can be seen in many well-preserved skulls, and the nerves associated with hearing passed through holes in the skull in the same places that they do in modern animals. All these things indicate that most dinosaurs probably had good hearing abilities. Small meat-eating dinosaurs like *Troodon* had special adaptations in the ear region that allowed them to accurately locate the direction from which sounds were coming. *Tyrannosaurus* and its closest relatives had adaptations that would have allowed them to hear lower frequencies of sound, possibly so they could pick out the low, bellowing "songs" of hadrosaurs and ceratopsians. Unlike mammals, dinosaurs did not have the fleshy ear lobes that are so obvious in mammals.

62. Did dinosaurs talk? Do we know what they sounded like? It is safe to assume that dinosaurs made sounds because their nearest living relatives (birds, which are dinosaur offspring, and crocodiles, which are dinosaur cousins) use their voices to communicate with each other. Beyond that, it is very difficult to determine how much most dinosaurs would have relied on sounds for communication. Many of the hadrosaurs had elaborate crests on top of their heads. Each crest enclosed the nasal passages, which extended from the nostrils through the crest to eventually open into the throat. Within the crest itself, these passages expanded into a large space that seems to have been used as a resonating chamber. Similar adaptations are found in trumpeter swans and howler monkeys, where the quality of sounds generated in the throat are changed and amplified. The crest shapes vary among the different species of crested duckbilled dinosaurs, as do the chambers inside them. Because the resonating chambers have different shapes, each hadrosaur species would have produced its own distinctive sounds. One scientist has tried to mimic the sounds made by different hadrosaurs by blowing through tubes with different shapes. The sound of a *Parasaurolophus*, for example, has been likened to an archaic German musical instrument called a Krummhorn. More recently, computers have been used to analyze the acoustic qualities of the chambers within the crests, although a lot more needs to be known before the results are conclusive.

63. Could dinosaurs smell things well?   The front part of the brain, the olfactory lobe, is used for analyzing smells, and was well developed in most dinosaurs. The presence of large chambers behind the nostrils, some of which had become very elongated, suggests that most dinosaurs made good use of their sense of smell. In the late 1980s, paleontologists started to use CAT scans, working with equipment in hospitals, to look at the inside of dinosaur skulls. A surprising discovery in *Nanotyrannus*, a small relative of *Tyrannosaurus*, was that there was an elaborate system of thin bony plates in the nasal chambers behind the nostrils. Similar structures in mammals are called turbinals, and are used for extending the areas of sensory tissue to improve the sense of smell. It would appear therefore that some, if not all, meat-eating dinosaurs could smell things very well.

64. How good were the eyes of dinosaurs?   Like modern animals, different dinosaurs would have had different capabilities of sight. Some dinosaurs were probably rather short-sighted, and would have relied more on their other senses. Other species of dinosaurs probably had sharp visual acuity. It seems that dinosaurs were mostly diurnal animals, that is, they tended to be more active in daylight hours than they were after nightfall. Polar dinosaurs would have had no choice during the summer months, when the sun never sets in the high latitudes. As animals of the daylight, they probably had color vision, just as their living relatives do today. Dinosaurs generally had large eye sockets, and in a few cases the scleral ring (a series of thin, platelike bones that form a circle within the iris of the eye much like the diaphragm of a camera lens) is preserved and shows that the eyeball was also large. The optic lobes of dinosaur brains are usually well developed, and support the idea that most dinosaurs had good vision. One suspects that animals that could raise their heads so far above the ground would also have had an advantage in being able to spot approaching enemies if their eyesight was good. Although all of these lines of reasoning are suggestive, none can provide conclusive evidence about the seeing abilities of any particular species of dinosaur.

65. Could dinosaurs see at night? Although most dinosaurs were probably active primarily during daylight hours, some were undoubtedly active during the night. *Troodon* and some of the other small meat-eating dinosaurs may have been like this. The evidence for this is rather scanty, and is based solely on the fact that their eyes were huge. For example, the diameter of the eyeball of *Dromaeosaurus* was almost a quarter the length of the skull. Although this dinosaur would have weighed less than an adult human, the diameter of its eyeball is about three times the size of a human eye. Among modern animals, those with the largest eyes, including cats and owls, tend to be nocturnal animals that rely on their night vision.

66. Could *Tyrannosaurus rex* see only moving prey, as suggested in *Jurassic Park*? Although some animals with relatively poor eyesight can only detect prey that is moving, it is unlikely that any dinosaurs had such a primitive level of sight discrimination. The eyesight of crocodilians and birds, the closest living relatives of dinosaurs, is generally good, and it is likely that dinosaurs were just as sophisticated. In the movie *Jurassic Park*, *Tyrannosaurus rex* was only able to detect the presence of another animal visually when it was moving. However, we would recommend that if you ever find yourself face to face with a *Tyrannosaurus rex*, do not stand in one place expecting the beast to move on!

67.   How could dinosaurs as large as a sauropod or a *Stego-saurus* have such small brains and still have survived in their world?   There is a lot that we do not know about intelligence in animals, although it is generally assumed that animals with smaller brains are less intelligent. This has led to the development of a number of misconceptions, including the legendary small brain of *Stegosaurus* and the incomparable stupidity of all dinosaurs. Even so, computers provide us with a valuable lesson because small home computers are only a fraction the size of computers of the 1960s, yet they are far faster, have a lot more memory and can perform many more functions. With computers, which can be considered as electronic or mechanical brains, big is not necessarily best. This may also have been true of sauropod brains. We know that sauropod dinosaurs had strong selective pressures working on them favoring the reduction of head size. Given the fact that most of the brain is not in active use, it may be relatively simple for an animal to reduce brain size without any loss of intelligence. It is quite clear that from the little we know about social behavior in sauropods, they had more complex behavior than we would expect from animals that had such small brains. It is also worth noting that stegosaurs did not have brains the size of walnuts. This was a misconception based on a cast of the inside of the braincase of a specimen where all of the rock had not been cleaned out. Although the brains of stegosaurs were small, they were relatively larger than those of sauropods.

68.   Could dinosaurs think?   Like many "lower" animals, dinosaurs probably did not have the capability of "weighing the consequences" before they actually did something. Most of their actions would probably be described as instinctive. Nevertheless, they probably had a capacity for learning from their mistakes, especially if those mistakes resulted in painful experiences. The largest-brained dinosaurs had brains within mammalian or avian size ranges, and these animals may have been capable of similar sorts of thought actions. Whether this can be considered as "thinking" or not cannot be determined at this time.

69. Did *Stegosaurus* really have a second brain in its hips?
In *Stegosaurus*, sauropods and some other dinosaurs, there was an expansion of the spinal cord within the sacral vertebrae of the hips. This ganglion or node was almost twenty times the size of the brain, and has often been referred to as the second brain. Similar spinal expansions can be found in a variety of modern animals, but are most common in migrating birds. They have nothing to do with a second point of controlling the body, and certainly had nothing to do with any thinking processes. The expansion simply is one of the many places in the body that is used for the storage of starches and fats that are used for food during long migrations or during other periods when food is difficult to obtain.

70. If one dinosaur stepped on the end of another dinosaur's tail, how long would it take for the nerve impulse to reach the brain? It was once a popular misconception that if something stepped on the end of a sauropod tail, it would take several minutes for the impulse to reach the brain. Another version of this myth is that if a dinosaur met a modern man with a high-powered rifle and was shot, it would take several minutes before it realized that it was dead. In other words, it would continue to attack long after it had been lethally wounded. Although we cannot calculate the transmission time of nerve impulses in animals that died out so long ago, there is no reason to believe that it was any different than in modern animals. These are invariably so fast as to suggest that signals would reach the brain of even the longest dinosaur in less than a second. And if there was incapacitating damage to the body, the dinosaur would be down, regardless of whether it knew why or not.

7. The World Dinosaurs Lived In

71. Which continents are dinosaurs found on? Dinosaurs have now been discovered on all continents, including Antarctica. This should not be surprising because at certain times in the history of the world, the continents were all connected to each other. Furthermore, the land masses on which dinosaurs lived have always been moving and changing their latitudes. The North American land mass was once found mostly south of the equator, and Antarctica has been far enough north to experience subtropical climates. During most of the history of the Earth, the polar regions were ice-free, and high-latitude climates would probably have been very pleasant for dinosaurs.

Asia and North America have produced the most dinosaur skeletons. This is mostly because these regions have had long histories of dinosaur hunting, whereas the other continents have been surveyed less intensively. In recent years, progressively more time has been invested in South America and Africa, which has resulted in the discovery of many new types of dinosaurs.

72. Was the whole world warm and tropical when dinosaurs were alive? Climates were generally warmer and less extreme when dinosaurs were the dominant land animals. The world today is actually much colder than it has been throughout most of its history. The ice caps that cover much of the Arctic and Antarctic regions have been around for less than three million years. Before that time, there was virtually no permanent ice locking up moisture. Without the polar ice caps, the sea levels were higher than they are today. Because much of North America, Asia and other continents were covered by broad, relatively shallow seas during Mesozoic times, the influences of warm tropical waters were felt deep into the polar regions. Few land areas were wide enough to have had "continental climates," and the climates worldwide were moderated by the ocean currents. Like today, tropical lowlands would have been unbearably hot in all seasons.

Dinosaurs have almost always been thought of by most people as tropical animals. This belief is based on equating dinosaurs with modern reptiles, most of which do live in the tropics. However, dinosaurs were very different from modern reptiles, and in many ways are more comparable to mammals and birds. The fossil record shows that the most diverse dinosaur faunas were to be found in warm temperate climatic regions, and extended all the way up into the polar latitudes. Because of their large body sizes, most dinosaurs probably had more problems with getting rid of excess body heat than they did with keeping warm. This made the tropics a difficult place for them to live in. The dinosaurs that did live in the tropics developed special adaptations for shedding excess body heat. These included the high, sail-like spines in animals like *Acrocanthosaurus*, *Ouranosaurus* and *Spinosaurus*. Because relatively few dinosaurs were able to inhabit tropical regions, the tropics acted as an effective barrier between Northern- and Southern-Hemisphere dinosaur faunas. Even though land connections existed between North and South America during the Cretaceous times, and hadrosaurs were able to move between the two continents, ceratopsians and most families of theropods failed to push south beyond the Equator.

73. Did dinosaurs live in the polar regions?   Dinosaurs from Alaska, Arctic Canada (the Yukon and Northwest Territories) and Siberia all lived within the Arctic Circle during Cretaceous times. Australia was much farther south than it is today, and when the dinosaurs of the southern coast of that continent were alive, they lived within the Antarctic Circle. This is also true of most of the dinosaurs that have been found in Antarctica. On the other hand, Greenland was once much farther south than it is today, and the dinosaurs found in its Triassic rocks actually lived at about the same latitude that Florida is today.

Even though it was not as cold in the polar regions during Mesozoic times as it is now, it was still dark all day during the winter months. Plants dropped their leaves and needles during the winters and became dormant. Without anything to eat, most dinosaurs were forced either to migrate toward the Equator or to hibernate. Although this may seem like a tough way to make a living, the polar summers, when the sun never set day or night, were incredibly productive for plants. The quantity and quality of plant food during the summer was what brought the dinosaurs into the polar regions.

74.　What kinds of environments did dinosaurs live in?
Dinosaurs were generally land-living animals, although their descendants the birds successfully invaded both the air and the seas before the majority of dinosaurs became extinct at the end of the Cretaceous. On land, however, dinosaurs successfully invaded just about every environment that was available to them. They lived in the tropics, the temperate regions and the polar regions. Some were adapted for life in coastal marshes and swamps, but the majority of dinosaurs preferred forests, open fern-covered plains, high-altitude basins in the mountains, hills, and even deserts.

75.　What kinds of plants lived at the same time as dinosaurs?
Plants, like animals, have been constantly evolving and changing over time. The plants that dominated the world at the end of the Triassic when dinosaurs first appeared were much more primitive than the ones at the end of the Cretaceous. Flowering plants (angiosperms) were well established worldwide long before the great extinction period when dinosaurs ceased to be the dominant land animals. It has even been suggested that angiosperms and some types of dinosaurs (hadrosaurs, ceratopsians) coevolved, and that neither could have become as successful without the presence of the other. Most major types of plants that are found in the world today had close relatives alive during Mesozoic times. The grasses, which did not appear until about fifty million years ago, are a notable exception.

76.　What kinds of animals lived on land at the same time as dinosaurs?　The world that dinosaurs lived in was not all that different from the modern world in many ways. Many of the smallest animals that dominate modern faunas also numerically dominated dinosaurian faunas. Most modern families of spiders and insects lived with dinosaurs, as did frogs, salamanders, turtles, lizards and crocodiles. Snakes and alligators had also appeared before the end of the Cretaceous. Birds took to the air by the end of the Jurassic and became diverse and numerous in the Cretaceous. Mammals appear in the fossil record at around the time that the first dinosaurs evolved in the Late Triassic. They became very numerous and diverse, but generally remained small and secretive until the large dinosaurs became extinct.

77.   Are there any places in the world today that look like the places dinosaurs lived in? In terms of both faunas and floras, a good way to imagine what most dinosaur sites in North America looked like during the Late Cretaceous would be to go to a warm temperate region like northern Florida. There were many diverse environments available for them to live in, including forests, marshes, swamps and savanna. The plants and most of the animals would have been much the same then as now, except that there were dinosaurs rather than large mammals, flying reptiles rather than large birds, and more ferns instead of grasses.

78.   If dinosaurs were brought back to life, could they survive in our world? Dinosaurs were perfectly adapted for their own world, which toward the end of the Cretaceous was not significantly different from many parts of the world today. Nevertheless, a lot of changes have taken place in the last 65 million years, and it is questionable whether a dinosaur would have the immunity necessary to combat modern diseases. Modern mammals are far more sophisticated than their ancestors that lived with the dinosaurs, and a Mesozoic dinosaur would probably have a difficult time competing with the large mammals that ultimately filled the ecological niches that were left vacant when dinosaurs became extinct.

8. Dinosaur Behavior

79. Would dinosaurs have behaved much differently from modern animals? Dinosaurs probably did not behave any differently from modern animals. Dinosaurs were living animals that obeyed all the "laws of nature." Complex life appeared more than a billion years ago, and dinosaurs (like mammals) were relative latecomers in the history of the world. Because of these two facts, it is unlikely that either dinosaurs or mammals have any behavioral attributes that had not been experimented with earlier by other types of animals. Many fish, amphibians and reptiles care for their young, "herding" is very common behavior in almost every major group of animals, migration is practiced in fish, insects and a host of other animals, and so on.

80. Did dinosaurs move in herds? There is strong evidence from trackway sites and bonebeds to show that many species of dinosaurs probably moved in herds. The best trackway sites for demonstrating this behavior have series of tracks going in predominantly one direction. One site in British Columbia actually shows that four animals were walking so close to each other that when one slipped, it affected the pathways of its three neighbors. Bonebeds sometimes document the mass deaths of single species herds of plant-eating dinosaurs. One herd of *Centrosaurus* from Alberta appears to have been decimated when it attempted to cross a river in flood, and a huge herd of *Maiasaura* from Montana may have been suffocated when volcanic ash rained down on them. Similar mass deaths have been documented for some species of prosauropods, sauropods, iguanodonts, stegosaurs, ankylosaurs and even some meat-eating theropods. Although not all dinosaurs were herding animals, clearly this type of behavior was as widespread during the Mesozoic era as it is today.

81. Did dinosaurs migrate? Many species of dinosaurs appear to have been herding animals, and one of the most common reasons that animals collect into herds today is to migrate from one area to another. It is quite clear that a herd of *Centrosaurus*, which consisted of several thousand individuals weighing up to four tons each, could not have stayed in any region for long before it ate all of the available food. Like large herding mammals, dinosaurs probably only collected into herds when they were ready to move to other areas. Once those areas were reached, the herds probably dispersed until it was time to move again. Dinosaurs living in the Arctic regions appear to have been likely candidates for this pattern of migratory behavior. During the winter months, many species would have opted to move south rather than stay in the land of perpetual winter darkness and no food. But every spring the same species would have migrated north again to take advantage of the high-quality food produced by twenty-four hours of daily sunshine in the summer.

82. Did dinosaurs take care of their young? It is very difficult to determine whether dinosaurs cared for their young or not. However, the presence of both babies and adults at nesting sites and in places where herds were destroyed by natural catastrophes strongly suggest that many dinosaurs did care for their young. A trackway site in Texas reveals that baby sauropods were surrounded by the adults when the herds were moving. And a nesting site in Montana seems to indicate that the babies remained in their nests after hatching, and were brought food by one or both of their parents. Parental care of young is a widespread phenomena in the animal kingdom, and is not restricted to birds and mammals. Even an animal as ferocious as a crocodile can be a gentle, protective parent to a newborn baby. But although many species of dinosaurs probably did take care of their young, this was not a universal tendency. Several adult *Coelophysis* skeletons have been collected with the remains of baby *Coelophysis* in their stomachs!

83. Did any dinosaurs have live babies? We normally think of mammals as the only animals that give birth to live young. However, a wide variety of modern animals as diverse as some species of spiders, fish, frogs and snakes do give birth to live young rather than laying eggs. In this way the adults are able to provide protection for a longer period of time, and the young are generally born larger and stronger than they would be if hatched from eggs. Among extinct reptiles, many fossils have demonstrated that the highly adapted swimming reptiles known as ichthyosaurs gave birth to live young. However, we do not know if there were any dinosaur species that did this. It has been suggested that some of the sauropods may have been live bearers, but the evidence for this hypothesis is circumstantial. In conclusion, it would not be surprising to learn that some species of dinosaurs gave birth to live young. But at this time there is no evidence to show that any dinosaur species did anything other than lay eggs.

84. What were the long tails of sauropods used for? The long, flexible tail has long been considered as the only line of defense for a sauropod. When one considers that the tail of *Seismosaurus* was close to 40 feet (12 meters) long, the energy produced at the end of the lashing tail would have been enough to cut a human in half. Consistent with this interpretation is the fact that many tails of sauropod skeletons have been damaged. More remarkable, perhaps, was the discovery that at least two types of sauropods from China (*Shunosaurus, Omeisaurus*) have clubs of bone on the ends of their tails. This certainly would have increased the amount of damage that a sauropod could inflict on any carnivore that dared to attack it.

85. Did ankylosaurs use the clubs on the ends of their tails for defense? The tails of some ankylosaurs of the family Ankylosauridae (including *Ankylosaurus, Euoplocephalus, Pinacosaurus, Saichania* and *Tarchia*) had defensive clubs that probably weighed more than 45 pounds (20 kilograms) when they were alive. They are not present in juvenile specimens, and even in young adults they are very small. The tail itself is stiffened by tendons that have turned to bone and have fused the last half of the tail into the club. The tail does not seem to have been strongly muscled, so it is unlikely that an ankylosaur could either raise or swing its tail. It is far more likely that they simply pivoted on their hind legs when they were attacked. This action would bring the tail around, and if the theropod happened to be in the way, it would get a very nasty bang on the shins.

86. Did ceratopsians use their horns to attack tyrannosaurs?

Ceratopsian horns probably served a variety of functions, including defense. First and foremost of these functions was visual identification. Differences in the shapes of the horns and frills of horned dinosaurs allowed them to identify potential mates and rivals. This is similar to the evolutionary strategy used by deer, cattle and antelope. The bulls with the biggest horns were probably able to attract the most females, and visually could scare off smaller bulls without having to fight. If fighting became necessary, the horns were oriented to interlock with the horns of the rival, again to minimize the amount of damage caused by fights between members of the same species. The horns would also have been effective in warding off the attacks of predatory dinosaurs. However, in most cases they were probably able to avoid this kind of confrontation. Tyrannosaurs would have fought and killed young, sick and old ceratopsians, but they were probably smart enough to avoid the horns of healthy, young adults.

9. Dinosaur Extinction

87. What was the last dinosaur? If one ignores for the moment the fact that birds are dinosaurs, there were relatively few dinosaurs that lived until the end of the Cretaceous. The fossil record is very poorly understood at the time boundary between the Cretaceous and Tertiary periods. Dinosaurs that lived up to the Cretaceous–Tertiary boundary in North America include *Anatotitan* (which at different times has been known as *Anatosaurus, Edmontosaurus [copei]* and *Trachodon), Ankylosaurus, Torosaurus, Triceratops* and *Tyrannosaurus.* Teeth and isolated bones of many other dinosaurs have been found in the same beds, but it is apparent that the diversity of dinosaurs had already been seriously reduced before they became extinct.

88. When did the last dinosaur die out? Because birds are dinosaurs, dinosaurs have not died out. The last dinosaur that is not a bird seems to have disappeared from the Earth about 65 million years ago. It is questionable whether or not the last dinosaurs became extinct everywhere in the world at the same time. Evidence from China, Montana, New Mexico, South America and a few other places suggests that some dinosaurs may have survived the Cretaceous–Tertiary extinction event.

89. Are dinosaurs extinct? Are there any dinosaurs alive today? In spite of reports that dinosaurs, plesiosaurs and other Cretaceous giants have been seen in the Congo, Loch Ness and many other remote corners of the Earth, it is highly unlikely that any of these animals are still alive today. Large animals would find it very difficult to escape discovery from humans, and this is compounded by the fact that they would need large populations and large home ranges to avoid extinction. Nevertheless, dinosaurs are still alive and very successful. Birds are the direct descendants of small meat-eating dinosaurs, and in modern biological classification are considered to be a subset of the Dinosauria. In this sense, dinosaurs are still very successful because there are more than 8,000 species alive today. This is approximately double the number of living mammalian species.

90. Did cavemen live at the same time as dinosaurs? What we normally consider as human beings appeared on the Earth less than five million years ago, whereas the last dinosaurs (except for birds) had all become extinct 65 million years ago. In other words, dinosaurs had died out more than 60 million years before the first human appeared. The only dinosaurs that humans have seen alive are those dinosaurian descendants we call birds.

91. Why did dinosaurs die out? Dinosaur extinction is one of the great unsolved mysteries of science. There have been hundreds of theories proposed to explain the great Cretaceous–Tertiary extinction event. However, so few people actually work on dinosaurs around the world that two very fundamental questions still have not been answered: (1) Did dinosaurs die out gradually or catastrophically? (2) Did the last dinosaurs disappear from the Earth at the same time on all continents?

One of the most popular theories of gradual extinction suggests that climatic changes eliminated dinosaurs over a period of several million years. In recent years, the most widely accepted extinction theory is that an asteroid collided with the Earth and set in motion a chain of events that wiped out virtually all large animals. There may not be a single cause for such widespread extinction. The authors of this book, for example, believe that the evidence suggests dinosaurs were gradually disappearing over several million years before the end of the Cretaceous. During this period, inland seas were withdrawing from North America, Asia and other regions. The seas had moderated the climates on land and, as they disappeared, climates became more continental: that is, seasonal and daily temperature differences became more extreme. The harsher climates caused a reduction in dinosaur diversity, thereby reducing their chances of survival when a major catastrophe happened 65 million years ago. That catastrophe seems to have come from outer space, and when the asteroid hit it threw enormous quantities of dust into the air. As the dust spread throughout the atmosphere, it shut out the sunlight and caused a collapse of entire ecosystems. Plants died because of a lack of sunshine, and without them, the plant-eating dinosaurs died out. This in turn caused the extinction of the meat-eating dinosaurs. Smaller animals were able to survive by eating seeds and other plant parts. Small meat-eaters survived by eating the small plant-eaters. But there was not enough food to sustain big animals, and the big dinosaurs were gone forever. Most plants recovered as seeds germinated and roots sprouted. But the world would never be the same.

92. Did other animals become extinct at the same time as the dinosaurs? Dinosaurs were not the only animals that became extinct at the end of the Cretaceous. All big animals died out, and a significant proportion of the small ones. Some calculations suggest that 75% of the species of animals on land and in the seas perished. Dinosaurs (except for the birds), ammonites, flying reptiles, mosasaurs, and plesiosaurs are just a few of the major groups of animals that disappeared forever from the face of the Earth. This was not the biggest extinction event in the planet's history, but almost all plants and animals were affected in some way. And out of the ashes, birds and mammals flourished and competed for the dominance of land and sea. Mammals eventually won in the sense that they became the largest, strongest herbivores and carnivores. But the dinosaurs we call birds maintained their numerical superiority over mammals.

10. The Study of Dinosaurs

93. What are scientists who work on dinosaurs called?
Paleontologists are scientists who specialize in the study of ancient life, including plants, invertebrates (animals without backbones) and all types of vertebrates (animals with backbones). Vertebrate paleontologists do their research on fish, amphibians, turtles, lizards, snakes, crocodiles, dinosaurs and mammals. In 1986, at a scientific meeting in Drumheller (Canada), the term dinosaurologist was proposed for scientists who work on dinosaurs. Scientists who work on one group of dinosaurs (birds) are referred to as ornithologists, or as paleo-ornithologists if they study fossil birds.

94. How do paleontologists know what dinosaurs looked like? Paleontologists get their information about how dinosaurs looked from studying both fossils and living animals. Dinosaur skeletons provide the general proportions, size and some indication of how they may have moved. Muscle scars (rough areas on the surfaces of bones) show where muscles attached and suggest how big or strong they would have been in the living animals. Many dinosaurs have been found with skin covering parts or all of their bodies. Trackways indicate how the animals were moving when they were alive, and even how they interacted with each other. Skin coloration is not known for any dinosaur. The understanding of living animals helps paleontologists identify and reconstruct anatomical features like bones, muscles, nerves and blood vessels. Paleontologists, and the artists who work with them, also need to be somewhat creative to fill in missing details. However, this creativity is held in check by the analyses of other scientists and by the discovery of new and better specimens.

95. Can a paleontologist reconstruct a whole dinosaur from just one bone? It is sometimes possible to know what a whole dinosaur looked like on the basis of one single bone, although scientists would never reconstruct skeletons for displays on such scanty material. Isolated dinosaur bones are much more common than complete dinosaur skeletons. It is relatively easy for a scientist to determine what part of the body any individual bone comes from. For example, the upper arm bones (humeri) of any vertebrate animal look very different from the upper leg bones (femora). Once it has been determined what part of the body a bone came from, it is possible to figure out what type of animal it came from. Some bones are very hard to identify because they look almost the same in a wide range of animals. In other cases the bones are so distinctive that they can be identified right down to species level. As another example, the humerus (upper arm bone) of a duckbilled dinosaur looks very different from the humeri of theropods, sauropods, horned dinosaurs and armored dinosaurs. However, the humeri of the duckbilled *Corythosaurus, Hypacrosaurus* and *Lambeosaurus* are similar enough that it would be very difficult to know which one of these three animals an isolated humerus came from unless there was additional information.

When an isolated dinosaur bone is found, it is identified as far as possible. If it is distinctive enough, it is possible to determine the species it represents. If that species is known from more complete specimens, possibly whole skeletons, then it would be possible to reconstruct the whole skeleton from just that one bone. This is never done, simply because it would be too much work, and it is easier and more productive to just go out and find more complete specimens.

96. Can a dinosaur be cloned if its DNA is found? Although many laboratories around the world are attempting to extract DNA (the genetic blueprint) from fossilized bones, blood (in fossilized biting insects preserved in amber) and eggs, it is highly unlikely that a dinosaur could be brought back to life. This is because only small pieces of the code are being recovered, and it would be like attempting to reconstruct a building from the corner of one page of the blueprints. Furthermore, it is not even possible yet to clone from the DNA of a living animal.

Scientists are not attempting to recover DNA from dinosaurs with the purpose of bringing a dinosaur back to life. DNA can be used to look at a level of detail not even dreamed of a few years ago, and comparisons made between the genetic material of different animals gives very accurate information on how those animals are related.

97. How many species of dinosaurs are there? Fewer than 800 species of dinosaurs (excluding birds) are known at this time. Although this may sound like a lot, it is a very low number considering they had a worldwide distribution and survived for more than 160 million years. Consider the fact that there are more than 8,000 species of birds, 6,000 species of amphibians and reptiles, and 4,000 species of mammals alive today. There are different ways to estimate how many species of dinosaurs might have lived during Mesozoic times, and these suggest that we have discovered less than a quarter of 1% to as much as 10% of the species that existed.

98. What are some of the "newest" dinosaurs that have been discovered? New dinosaurs are being discovered and described all of the time. For example, new meat-eating dinosaurs have been found in the last decade on every continent, and include the following species.

Afrovenator is a large theropod from Niger, Africa. It looked similar to the well-known *Allosaurus* from North America.

Baryonyx was a long-snouted, fish-eating theropod. An almost complete skeleton of this strange animal was discovered in England.

Cryolophosaurus was found only a few hundred miles from the South Pole. There was an unusual transverse crest above the eyes of this large meat-eater.

Eoraptor is a small theropod from Argentina. It is the most primitive theropod presently known, which is not surprising considering that it lived more than 225 million years ago.

Sinraptor, from northwestern China, was a 22-foot (7-meter) long predator that was similar to the first dinosaur described, *Megalosaurus*.

Timimus is an Australian ornithomimid that was first described in 1994.

Utahraptor, as its name suggests, was discovered in Utah. This raptor is related to *Dromaeosaurus* and *Velociraptor*, but is considerably larger.

99. If I wanted to work on dinosaurs, how long would I have to stay in school? There are different ways that people can work on dinosaurs, and each requires a different combination of education and skills. Some of the earliest and most successful dinosaur hunters had virtually no formal education. However, times have changed. In order to get a job as a dinosaur researcher in a museum or university, it is almost mandatory to have a doctorate (Ph.D) in North America. This usually means 12 years of primary and secondary schooling, another 4 years for a Bachelor of Science degree, 2 years for a Master of Science degree and at least 3 years for a Ph.D. Although this sounds like a long time, you will actually be doing research long before your education is completed. Most people consider their university years as the best time of their lives, and the ultimate goals are highly satisfying careers.

100. Are there many scientists in the world who work on dinosaurs? How much more is there to be learned about dinosaurs? There are surprisingly few people working on dinosaurs professionally. About 30 scientists worldwide have full-time paid positions to collect and do research on dinosaurs. There are many more scientists who have other specialties but work at least part time on dinosaurs, and students who are training to be dinosaurologists. However, even if one counts all of these positions, fewer than 150 people are undertaking original research on dinosaurs. The amount of money spent annually on all aspects of dinosaurian research is less than a million dollars. To put this in perspective, the movie *Jurassic Park* grossed close to a billion dollars in less than two years.

There is so much left to be learned about dinosaurs that it is fair to say that scientists have only removed a few glassfuls from a very deep well of knowledge. After studying dinosaurs for more than 150 years, considerably less than 10% of dinosaur species have been discovered. Most aspects of their biology, including whether or not they were warm-blooded, remain either unknown or controversial. And one of the greatest mysteries, the cause of the great extinction of 65 million years ago, remains unsolved in spite of some very promising leads.

101. Why is it important to study dinosaurs? There are many reasons to justify doing research on dinosaurs. They were one of the most successful life forms on this planet, and outcompeted mammals for more than 160 million years. Although large dinosaurs disappeared 65 million years ago, more than 8,000 species of small dinosaurs (which we call birds) are alive today. Our interest in the future of humanity makes us curious about why the large dinosaurs suddenly became extinct after dominating the world for so long. Dinosaur studies give us a historical understanding of the world that not only helps us keep our own position in nature in perspective, but gives us a better understanding of why things are the way they are now.

Commercially, dinosaurs have always been a huge success, attracting visitors to museums and amusement parks, and generating many millions of dollars in revenue every year through the sale of books, films, games, toys and so much more. Dinosaurs are a cultural phenomenon, and have become the heroes and villains of books, cartoons, comics and movies, the subjects of paintings and sculptures, the inspiration for songs and dances, and even the symbols for sports teams and commercial products. They are an educational tool from primary schools to universities, and are often used as vehicles for introducing science to students or for inspiring creativity in children. But for most of us who work on dinosaurs, we study them simply because they are such interesting creatures.

DOVER BOOKS ON MATHEMATICAL & LOGICAL PUZZLES, CRYPTOGRAPHY, AND WORD RECREATIONS

(continued on back flap)